FAMILY ENVIRONMENT, HA[illegible]
OF INDIVIDUALS LI[illegible]
AND NUCLEAR FAMILY

KOMAL RAJNIKANT VYAS

INDEX

CHAPTER- 1

INTRODUCTION

1.1 Introduction

1.2 Definition of Family

1.3 Definition of Family Environment

Dimensions of Family Environments

1.4 Definition of Happiness

Factors of Happiness

1.5 Definition of Personal Values

Type of personal Values

1.6 Summary

1.1 INTRODUCTION:

India has its own cultural significance in the whole world. A strong and prominent family system like India not found in any other countries. The Indian family system has a strong structure in the society with great importance. There have been many changes in the Indian family system in the present times but they have not been destroyed. According Dr.Akshay kumar Desai In traditional Indian society, the family was a unit of various oriented production and consumption. The family system was made up of blood relatives.

Everything has changed in the present times. The direct effect of his family is seen on the person. The complete development and growth of a person depends on his family. A person's perception of his family comes from the place he is in society. The family plays a part in the complete development of each individual. With the cooperation of the family person can make the expected tasks successful. The family provides support to the individual in every situation. Happiness, sorrow, success, failure, the family of a person plays an important role in all these. So family is most important for every person. Everyone is given a prominent place and right in the family system.

In recent times the definition of joint family, nuclear family as well as families living in villages and families living in cities has changed. In ancient times the Joint family had emotional bond between generations and they always used to stand together in the need of time. There was passing of traditions and cultural information to the successors which made them remember the importance of 'Collectivism' as a predominant social value vice a versa nuclear family sought after the principle of 'Individualism'.

Right now we are going through a difficult time of covid-19. Many have lost loved ones during this time. Many have lost their entire families. Living life as a single person in such a time is so much difficult. The whole life of any person is spent in the human community. The whole life is spent especially among one's own family. The family provides every opportunity for everyone to live life. In pandemic time many joint families have been transformed into nuclear family and many nuclear families have been transformed into joint family. In pandemic time a person who has lost his loved ones needs warmth, love, and consolation. The form and concept of the family has changed during this time. But a person cannot forget the importance of family in his/her life. Let his/her family be with him/her in every occasion of life.

In pandemic time we heard that in the news many individuals lost their jobs, business employment collapsed, Young children stopped playing, wedding occasions stopped, School colleges closed. There was a lot of trouble in big families about how to run a house. As a result of this confusion, many family members committed mass suicide. As the men stayed at home, they became addicted, the temper began to deteriorate. The workload of women in the family increased. Taking care of children and husbands as well as other members of the household throughout the day disrupts the physical and mental health of women. There were many effects of covid-19 in the village and in the city. The effect of covid-19 on each family was different.

Only a person's family can support him in such a time of trouble. This is the time when family's exam is held. That's how they get out of trouble.

1.2 DEFINITION OF FAMILY:

The family is an intimate domestic group made up of people related to one another by bonds of blood, sexual mating or legal ties. It is the smallest and most basic social unit, which is also the most important primary group found in any society.

It is the simplest and most elementary group found in a society. It is a social group consisting of a father, mother and one or more children. It is the most immediate group a child is exposed to. In fact, it is the most enduring group, which has tremendous influence on the life of an individual, from birth until death. It also accounts for the most enduring social relationship found in society. Family has been defined by different social scientists.

According to Sociologists, the family is **an intimate domestic group of people related to one another by bonds of blood, sexual mating, or legal**

ties. ... The family acts as a primary socialization of children whereby the child first learns the basic values and norms of the culture they will grow up in.

Family is a group defined by sexual relationship, sufficiently precise and enduring to provide for the procreation and upbringing of children.'– Maclver

'The family, almost without question, is the most important of any groups that human experience offers … the family … is with us always, or more precisely, we are with it.' – Robert Bierstedt

Family is a more or less durable association of husband and wife, with or without child, or of a man or woman alone, with children.'– M. F. Nimkoff

'Family is the biological social unit composed of husband, wife and children.' – Eliot and Merrill

Family is a group of persons united by ties of marriage, blood or adoption constituting a single household interacting and inter-communicating with each other in their respective social roles of husband and wife, father and mother, son and daughter, brother and sister, creating a common culture.'– Burgess and Locke

'Family is a group of persons, whose relations to one another are based upon consanguinity and who are therefore kin to one another.' – Kingsley Davis

1.2.1 Characteristics of Family

Family is a Universal group. It is found in some form or the other, in all types of societies whether primitive or modern.

A family is based on marriage, which results in a mating relationship between two adults of opposite sex.

Every family provides an individual with a name, and hence, it is a source of nomenclature.

Family is the group through which descent or ancestry can be traced. υ Family is the most important group in any individual's life.

Family is the most basic and important group in primary socialization of an individual.

1.2.2 Functions of Family

Family provides an individual with an identity.

It is through the family that every family name is carried on from one generation to another.

Family is responsible for the production and upbringing of children. Family is an important agent of socialization. The primary socialization of any individual takes place within the family. The immediate family members teach all the basic rules and norms of social life to a child.

A family fulfills the economic needs of its members. This function has undergone transformation, with families moving from being production and consumption units in earlier times, to becoming more of consuming units rather than a producing one.

1.2.3 Type of Family

1. Based on birth (Family orientation & Family procreation)
2. Based on Marriage (Monogamous Family, Polygynous Family, polyandrous Family
3. Based on Residence (Family of patrilocal residence, Family of Changing residence,
4. Based on Ancestry or Decent (Matrilineal Family, Patrilineal Family)
5. Based on Authority (Matriarchal Family, Patriarchal Family)
6. Based on the Nature of Relations (Conjugal Family, Consanguine Family)
7. Based on State or Structure (Nuclear Family and Joint Family)

- **Nuclear Family:**

A family consisting of two parents and their children, but not including aunts, uncles, grandparents, etc. In the western world the word "nuclear family" was used to differentiate between the family community composed primarily of parents, father or mother, and their offspring. Nuclear families can be of any scale, provided that the family may sustain itself and only parents and children are present.

The word "nuclear" has its original Latin sense, "kernal" or "nut." The move from joint structures to nuclear family systems was largely endorsed by the propagation of western ideals. Traditional family responsibilities shift as egalitarian values enter the social structure. It was believed historically that the guy was the protector of the household and the housewife was recorded in stone. Women still operate in significant numbers regardless of economic need. This is why conventional joint marriages split apart into nuclear families.

Pauline Kolenda (1987) has discussed additions/modifications in nuclear family structure. She gives the following compositional categories.

i) **Nuclear family** refers to a couple with or without children.

ii) **Supplemented nuclear family** indicates a nuclear family plus one or more unmarried, separated, or widowed relatives of the parents, other than their unmarried children.

iii) **Sub nuclear family** is identified as a fragment of a former nuclear family for instance a widow/widower with her/his unmarried children or siblings (unmarried or widowed or separated or divorced) living together.

iv) Single person household

v) **Supplemented sub nuclear family** refers to a group of relatives, members of a formerly complete nuclear family along with some other unmarried, divorced or widowed relative who was not a member of the nuclear family. For instance, a widow and her unmarried children may be living together with her widowed mother-in-law. In the Indian context, it is easy to find all these types of family. However, in terms of societal norms and values, these types relate to the joint family system.

- **Joint Family:**

A joint family consists of three generation, living together under the same roof, sharing the same kitchen and purse or economic expenses. It is a family consisting of three nuclear families living together. According to Iravati

Karve, a joint family is 'a group of people, who generally live under the same roof, who eat food cooked at one hearth, who hold property in common, and who participate in common family worship and are related to each other as some particular type of kindered.'

Pauline Kolenda (1987: 11-2) presents the following types of joint family on the basis of the relatives who are its members.

a) Collateral joint family: It comprises two or more married couples between whom there is a sibling bond. In this type, usually a brother and his wife and another brother and his wife live together with unmarried children.
b) Supplemented collateral joint family: It is a collateral joint family along with unmarried, divorced or widowed relatives. The supplemented relatives are generally the widowed mother of the married brothers or the widower father, or an unmarried sibling.
c) Lineal joint family: Two couples, between whom there is a lineal link, like between a parent and his married son or some times between a parent and his married daughter, live together.
d) Supplemented lineal joint family: It is a lineal joint family together with unmarried, divorced or widowed relatives who do not belong to either of the lineally linked nuclear families; for example, the father's widower brother or the son's wife's unmarried brother or sister.
e) Lineal collateral joint family: In this type three or more couples are linked lineally and collaterally. For instance we can have a family consisting of parents and their two or more married sons together with the unmarried children of the couples.
f) Supplemented lineal - collateral joint family: In this type are found a lineal collateral joint family plus unmarried, widowed, separated relatives who belong to one of the nuclear families (lineally and collaterally linked), for example, the father's widowed sister or brother or an unmarried nephew of the father.

1.3 DEFINITION OF FAMILY ENVIRONMENT:

The English word 'family' was derived from the Latin word 'familia', which refers to the household of individuals living together. 'Family' refers to "a group of individuals living together during important phases of their life time and bound to each other by biological and/or social and psychological relationship" **(B.B.Sethi, 1989).** According to the **UNESCO Report, 1992** "Family is a kinship unit and that even when its members do not share a common household, the unit may exist as a social reality". Down the ages the traditional Indian family structure has gone through several changes. **Aneesa Mohamed (2019),** on the basis of structure identifies three types of Indian family structure: Nuclear family, Joint family and Extended family. 'Family Environment' refers to the atmosphere that prevails at home. "Family Environment refers to the quality and quantity of cognitive, emotional and social support that has been available to the child within the family and connotes the psychological environment of family as perceived by adolescents". **(Bhatia and Chadha, 2004).** Love and mutual help will enhance the abilities of children, but loss of affection and neglect will exert negative influence on children

Family is the primary unit Members of the family lives together. The Family environment is most important to become a person to include in society. It has so many functions to develop of its members, their security and welfare. Therefore an individual is taken care by the family. Family environment is a unique thing each family made a different individual in a different perspective. Family environment is effected by so many factors like marital association between parents, members of the family, Socio-economic status of family, religion, and place of living of the family i.e., rural, urban.

Family environment surrounding means the atmospheric condition and around the home where one lives. It refers to various aspects of people's domestic lives that contribute to their living condition and their behaviour. It includes social, physical and emotional environment. It means the surrounding and everything which influences an individual at home. Family environment consists of social and economic status of the family, number of siblings, facilities available at home, attitude of the parents and children interaction etc. All these factors in a combined way constitute the Family environment.

Family environment is the core of all other social organizations. The family cooperation's assume a vital part in the advancement of a person. The sound working of these collaboration designs improves emotional well-being of the person. There are some vital interactional impacts amongst family and its individuals at various formative stages. It impacts the entire existence of the immature. It is the essential and imperative social condition to which a pre-adult is uncovered. A positive, steady, passionate bond between the family and youthful is an essential defensive element for their wellbeing and improvement. An unmistakable and unambiguous comprehension of parts with regards to family capacities is essential in moulding the immature. Analysts have reliably demonstrated that both general family framework working and parental practices are emphatically identified with youthful prosperity **(Grotevant, 1998; Karavasilis et al., 2003; Muris et al., 2004; Wolfradt et al., 2002).**Consciously, or unwittingly the home environment shape the conduct, identity, and disposition, level of desire, fitness, confidence and increment frustration tolerance level of the juvenile

The term "family" refers to a variety of groupings including (1) a father, mother and their children, (2) children of father and mother, (3) a group of people living in the same house,(4) all of a person's relatives, (5) a group of related people, (a) a tribe, (7) one's ancestors (Adams, 1975; Blood, 1972; Winch, 1971). According to Oxford Dictionary it is (a) the body of persons who live in one house with parents, children etc, (b) the ground consisting of parents and their children, (c) a person's children reared collectively, (d) those descended from a common ancestry

The family is human society's oldest, most basic and fundamental entity. It is a social institution that conveys our social heritage through it. Most of what we used to call heritage is simply the family's influence. Traditionally, the family is seen as the underlying pillar of society. Families can usually be seen as a group of individuals with biological, emotional or legal links to each other. It is well known that it is the most significant element that influences our thinking and attitudes by far. **Tiwari (1998)** states that family environment is, "the most important agent that influences the child's relationship with family."

According to Clare (2003) "family we mean a system of relationship existing between parents and children." "The family constitutes an interpersonal social system held together by strong bond of attachment, affection, care and yet exercises control, approval and discipline on each other's actions "" **(Harvey & Byrd, 2000; Parke & Buriel, 1998).**

Newman and Newman (1981) "Family environment is the first and perhaps the most enduring context for growth. Adjustment within family means identifying with models, accepting values and playing out family roles."

Ranhotra (1996) "Family environment is the complex of social and cultural conditions, the combination of extrinsic physical conditions that effect and influence the growth and development of the family."

According to Maclver and Page, (2006). "The family environment is a group defined by sex relationship sufficiently precise and enduring to provide for the procreation and upbringing of children" **while Clark (2007)** said, "by family environment, we mean a system of relationship existing between Parents and children." Family Environment basically mean: 1. The family is the main setting for the experiences of the child, particularly the young child. 2. The family is a dynamic set of relationships among all the people who live in the "family." 3. Children's behavior, ideas, thoughts, and fantasies affect the lives of those with whom they live. 4. The behavior, ideas, thoughts and fantasies of father and mother affect the lives of their children. 5. This group has resources that are used to adjust in life.

"The family is the only socially recognized relation for child bearing and the essential agency for child rearing, socialization, and introducing the child to the culture of the society, thereby shaping the basic character structure of our culture and forming the child's personality." **(Frank, 1948).**

Learning is a continuous process. It begins at birth and continues throughout the life. The family, as an institution is universal. It is the most permanent and the most pervasive of all social institutions. All type of societies whether it may be large or small, primitive or civilized, ancientor modern; have some form of family or the other. No one knows, or can know, how or when the family institution began. It is better to summaries that the family is some form will always be with us. With regards to the future as the mind can imagine the family will continue to be a control and indeed a nuclear component of society. Parents are the first teachers of their children. So, there is strong influence of them on their life. Since a child's environment is centered around his family initially, the family environment becomes the primary agent of socialization. The term "family environment" includes the circumstances and social climate conditions within the family. As composition of each family is different; so, family environment differ in many ways. Every family environment is unique. Some families live luxurious life while others have low socioeconomic status. The family environment is strongly related to individual's well-being.

The word family is derived from Latin word „**Famulus**" which means a servant. In Roman law, the word denoted a group of producers and slaves and other servants as well as members connected by common descent or marriage. Hence originally, a family consisted of a man and women with a child or children and servants. Family is a biological social unit, more or less durable association of husband, wife and children.

According to **Business Dictionary**," Family is a social unit of two or more persons related by blood, marriage, or adoption and having a shared commitment to the mutual relationship"

According to **Oxford Dictionary**, "A group consisting of two parents and their children living together as a unit."

According.to **All word Dictionary (2006),** "The family environment was based on social, physical and biological sciences and humanity.

- According to **Maclver and Page (2006),** "The family environment is a group defined by sex relationship sufficiently precise and enduring to provide for the procreation and upbringing of children."
- According to **Clark (2007),** "By family environment, we mean a system of relationship existing between Parents and children."

According to **Bjornberg & Nicholson, (2007)**, the assessment of family environments is usually based on dimensions like cohesion, support, conflict and hierarchy. Cohesion is an emotional bond that connects family members, which means sharing affection, friendship and intimacy. There is a perception of maternal and emotional support from the family in facing support challenges and problems; it may also be the presence of close, caring and acceptance among a teenager and his caregiver **(Barrow, Schuckit, Lucht, John & Frewyberger, 2002).** Conflicts involve a set of negative emotions among individuals, which can create tension, hostility, criticism, aggression with the family. After this, it follows that a teenager who experienced a general, supportive and well-integrated house, school, life took it to its fullest integration of all other associations and attitudes. **While Moos & Moos (2002)** concluded that adolescents living in assisted and organized families show the experience of marriage, confidence, social ability, less anxiety, less psychological health, and compare those of happy, harmonious parents. Do more good in Divorced or married distressed family. Psychological adjustment is the behavioral process through which man maintains a balance between his various requirements or the barrier between his needs and the environment. Psychological adjustment can be determined by asking the person about his feeling, attitude and cognitive, behavioral characteristics, because only according to **Peterson (2005)** he can assess the degree of experience of adjustment and satisfaction

"A group of people related by blood or marriage". The infant begins his life under the fostering affection and care of his parents and other near and dear ones who are associated with the family. As he grows, he learns the first lesson of life from his family and tries to adapt the habits, ideals and patterns of behaviour of his family members. In this way, family continuously influences him throughout his life. For the upbringing of an individual, there is no better institution than the family. Families in general and parents in particular, have often been deemed to be the most important support system available to the child. The strongest factor in moulding a child's personality or behavior is his relationship with his parents. Family environment affects how children have grown up. Good parents can grow their children successfully. Couples would have children someday, but they must have a plan about when they want children and how many children they want. In this world, there are many couples who are not prepared for it and bring children by accident. By it, they ignore their responsibility as a parent and not treated their children in proper way.

Family environment is the general and emotional atmosphere in a family. At times, the emotional climate may be difficult to perceive as it, truly exists. There is an interpersonal relationship among family members on the directions of personal growth emphasized in the family and on the structure of the family. Family environment mainly measures the three domains of thc family climate. The relationship dimension, personal growth or goal orientation dimension and system in maintenance and change dimension **(Anna, 2003).**

A family environment has strong effect on the overall well-being of an individual. The conditions of a family very much affect the livelihood and working way of an individual. A sense of belonging is felt from the strong bond of family. Families shape personality, develop personality, emotional strength, and work as a support system for all individuals. Individuals are not just moulded within this sociological unit i.e. family, for the preparation for routine experience but also determine how he/she will react to stressful experiences. Dysfunctional families often lead to individuals in making poor choices in life causing stress.

The family environment consists of family members, their attributes. Their personality, their behavior, their inter relationships. Along with these family environments also consists of; the physical appearance of house, home facilities, ventilation, the quality nutrition, family hygiene, parental education, parental occupation, their income, their living standard etc. A congenial environment in a family develops personality wholesomely whereas the stresses strains and evil activities of a broken family destroy one‟s development. It is the duty of each and every member of the family to pay due respect to the individuality of the child and foster in him a sense of belongingness and responsibility towards his own self and others. Because each family has its own culture and set up which is quite distinct from the other, therefore no two children are the same neither in the beginning, nor during development or as a growing up adult citizens.

1.3.1 Dimensions of Family Environment

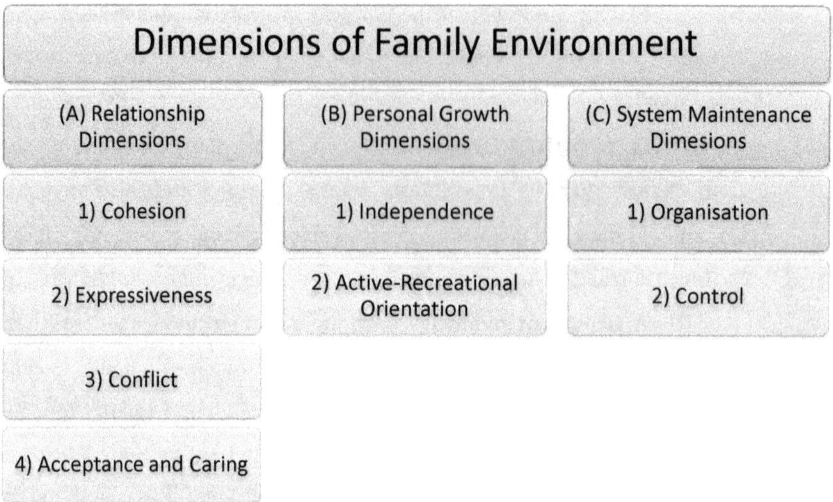

(A) Relationship Dimensions

1. **Cohesion -** Degree of Commitment , Help and Support Family Members Provide for One Another
2. **Expressiveness-** Extent to Which Family Members are Encouraged to Act Openly and Express Their Feelings and Thoughts Directly.

3. **Conflict-** Amount of Openly Expressed Aggression and Conflict Among Family Members.
4. **Acceptance and Caring-** Extent to Which the Members are Unconditionally Accepted and the Degree to Which Caring is expressed in the Family.

(B) Personal Growth Dimensions

5. **Independence-** Extent to Which Family Members are Assertive and Independently Make Their Own Decisions.
6. **Active- Recreational Orientation-** Extent of Participation in Social and Recreational Activities.

(C) System Maintenance Dimensions

7. **Organization** – Degree of Importance of Clear Organization Structure in Planning Family Activities and Responsibilities.
8. **Control** – Degree of Limit Setting Within a Family.

1.4 DEFINITION OF HAPPINESS:

Happiness is a positive emotional state. It involves the detailed evaluation of one's current position in the world. It is the sum total of positive effect and general life satisfaction. It is flourishing of human beings and associated with living a life of virtue. The happiness level of a person is governed by three factors which are a set point for happiness, happiness relevant circumstantial factors, and happiness-producing activities and practices. There are two traditions on happiness. They are eudemonic and hedonic.

Happiness is an emotional state characterized by feelings of joy, satisfaction, contentment, and fulfillment. While happiness has many different definitions, it is often described as involving positive emotions and life satisfaction.

Happiness is that feeling that comes over you when you know life is good and you can't help but smile. It's the opposite of sadness.

Happiness is a sense of well-being, joy, or contentment. When people are successful, or safe, or lucky, they feel happiness. The "pursuit of happiness" is something this country is based on, and different people feel happiness for different reasons. Whenever doing something causes happiness, people usually want to do more of it. No one ever complained about feeling too much happiness.

Happiness is ultimate goal of human life. Every human being aspires to live happy life throws his activities at work as well as family life.

Human well-being as a concept encompasses a well-rounded balanced and comprehensive experience of life. It includes health in social, physical, mental, emotional, career and spiritual domains. It can be thought of both as an outcome for which individuals strive and as a part of a functional process that helps an individual's to achieve their goals (**Lucas &Diener, 2008).**

Happiness is a nebulous term, which to date has different meanings to different people. To some it is synonymous with "Joy" while others accept the standard dictionary definition that happiness is a state of well-being or contentment –a condition dominated by pleasurable satisfaction **(Rahman.2006.)**

Seligman's conclusion is that happiness has three dimensions that can be cultivated: **the Pleasant Life, the Good Life, and the Meaningful Life**. The Pleasant Life is realized if we learn to savour and appreciate such basic pleasures as companionship, the natural environment and our bodily needs.

According to Aristotle, **happiness consists in achieving**, through the course of a whole lifetime, all the goods — health, wealth, knowledge, friends, etc. — that lead to the perfection of human nature and to the enrichment of human life. This requires us to make choices, some of which may be very difficult.

According to Oxford English dictionary, happiness is The state of pleasurable contentment of mind; deep pleasure in or contentment with one's circumstances.

According to Layard (2007; 2005) some people think that happiness is the ultimate goal of their life, instead Chekola (2007) claims that it is only one component of a good life. Although each person defines happiness based on his or hers own terms, in general people advocate similar things that make them happy (Conceição and Bandura, 2008; Lyubomirsky et al, 2005; Layard, 2005; Easterlin, 2001). Frey and Stutzer (2002; 2000) grouped happiness in demographic and personality factors (personality traits, gender, age, education, family and social environment, work,faith) in micro-macroeconomic (income, unemployment, inflation) and institutional ones. Mroczek and Kolarz(1998) believe that there is a positive relationship between age and happiness. Others claim that the relationship is U shaped, where happiness is higher in younger and third age (Blanchflower, 2009; Blanchflower and Oswald, 2004;Oswald, 1997) and others that there is no relationship (Easterlin, 2003; Myers, 2000).

There is a broad variation in how happiness is defined. According to MerriamWebster dictionary, happiness is (1) a state of well-being and contentment or (2) a pleasurable or satisfying experience (Merriam-Webster, 1995). However, researchers in the field have no agreed-upon definition of happiness. For example, Veenhoven (1997) suggested that happiness is a situation of one's mind that relates to the assessment of one's whole life in total. Norrish and Vella-Brodrick (2008) posit that happiness is not only about the satisfaction about one's life in general, but it is also associated with one's psychological change of increasing positive aspects while decreasing negative aspects. Additionally, some scholars use happiness interchangeably with other words or phrases. For example, Easterlin (2003) substituted happiness with terms like utility, well-being or life satisfaction. Mroczek and Kolarz (1998) saw happiness as equal to well-being. At the same time, there were also some systematic explanations about happiness. For instance, when Diener et al. (1999) summarized the components of Subjective Well Being (SWB), they categorized happiness as "pleasure affects," one of the major components of Subjective Well Being. Based on a review of the literature, Shin and Johnson (1978) also suggested that happiness could mean (1) a pure feeling of people (e.g. feeling happy); (2) the expression or assessment about a situation (e.g. be happy with something) and (3) an 6 assessment of one's whole life (e.g. being happy). The definition of happiness has long been discussed in theoretical works and various empirical studies from various academic fields such as philosophy, psychology and sociology. Nonetheless, one can still find one or two popular conceptualizations in happiness studies in general such as "life satisfaction" and "positive affect."

1.4.1 Factors of Happiness

(I). Subjective Well-being

SWB is defined as: Satisfaction with Life + High Positive Affect + Low Negative Affect. Life Satisfaction Encompasses the Cognitive Component of Happiness When Individuals Rate the Way Their Life Turns Out to be. Affect refers to the emotional side of well-being, including moods and emotions associated with experiencing momentary events (Diener et. Al., 1999). People who demonstrate higher levels of SWB tends to demonstrate higher levels of creativity , increased task persistence, multitasking, being systematic, optimism, attending to relevant negative information; longevity, less vulnerable to illness, trust helpfulness, and less self-centeredness.

(II). Social Well-being

It represents your relationships and experiences of love. Recognizing emotions in others, where one has the ability to exhibit empathy, which is important for social relationships.

(III). Emotional Well-being

It is where one is able to identify and understand one's own emotions. Experiencing fewer negative emotions but a similar number of positive emotions and develop greater emotional complexity (example, joy and sadness can be inter mixed at the same moment), enhancing mood, health (fewer illness and visits to doctors), insight and self examination.

(iv). Career Well-being

This represents where you spend most of your time during the day. How constructively and Satisfactorily one spends their day in major activities.

(v) Spiritual Well-being

People who report themselves as being spiritual or religious tend to report slightly higher levels of Well-being, in addition to higher scores on hope and optimism. Connecting to something permanent and important that can give comfort, meaning and sense of identity.

1.5 DEFINITION OF PERSONAL VALUES:

India is a country of values. Values are guiding stars which guide the path of the human being to choose the right alternative. Value means something which has a price, something precious, dear and Mittal 204 worthwhile; hence something one is ready to suffer and sacrifice for. Values are a set of principles or standards of behavior **(Dhinakaran, V. and Sivakumar, R., 2014). According to Davidov, Schmidt and Schwartz (2008)** values are defined "as deeply rooted, abstract motivations that guide, justify or explain attitudes, norms, opinions and actions". In the words of **Surinder**

(2012), "value is an intrinsic truth. It is an essential norm and governs the moral universe of man"

Values play the supreme role in the making of the individual, society as well as a nation. Behavior and conduct of an individual largely depends on his values. Values shape his character and personality. Signifying the role of values **Kaur, J. and Kaur, H. (2013)** stated that values are those principles which guide human behavior and put meaning to his existence. Values form the central pole around which people organize their desire and ambitions and fashion their idioms of life. Values affect the feelings, emotions, thoughts, and attitude and in this way influence the decisions and behavior of the individual. Values play an important role in the motivation of a person's behavior **(Indira, K., 2009).**

Personal values are originated from the external circumstances. Values can also be changed over time. Honesty in the application of values is referred to its continuity. Individual is said to have integrity if s/he applies her/his values appropriately regardless of positive or negative reinforcement from others. It would be appropriate to apply religious values in times of happiness as well as in times of despair.

Personal values are absolutely related to choice of an individual. These values actually guide the individual in taking decisions. Personal values are developed from early life and it is also resistant to be easily altered. These personal values are derived from culture, religion, and political identity. However, personal values are not universal. Personal values of an individual are determined by the genes, family, nation, historical environment etc. The concept of values is not universal. Values vary from individual to individual and from group to group.

Kohn (1969) has defined value as desirable. Trans-situational goal's ranging in importance as guiding principles in people's lives again. According to **Inglehart (1990)** there are ten types of values – power, achievement, hedonism, stimulation, self-direction, universalism, benevolence, tradition, conformity and security. These value types encircle specific individual values.

Ganguli(1989)has said that in india in accordance with the ancient tradition, the spiritual values are embedded with religions: and philosophy can claim to be the primary and original source of all desired social values.

According to **Garg et al (2006)** spiritual attitude and activities are positively related to knowledge, health as well as power values, balance, adjustment and feeling of usefulness.

Ocholla (1997) has opined that individuals lie between two situations – (a) the traditional one which supplies customs, ethics, social values, religious hopes, and (b)modern way of life of education, transport, communication and political debate.

Inglehart (1997) has exhibited that older persons in much of the world give higher priority to materialist vs. post-materialist values than younger people. He has interpreted this as a cohort effect. People form values in adolescence that change little thereafter.

A value is a conviction, a mission, or a philosophy that is meaningful. Whether we are consciously aware of them or not, every person has a core or personal values (PV). Values can range from the conviction in hard work and regularity, as well as other psychological, such as, self-reliance, apprehension for others, and congruence of persistence. Values reproduce the power of action and its consequences. The more it express, the greater its power and effectivity. Personal values that are experienced by individuals are ranked higher in order than the social values which seem abstract or impersonal. In practical life, personal values play a very effective role

Personal values evolve from circumstances with the external world and can change over time. Integrity in the application of values refers to its continuity; persons have integrity if they apply their values appropriately regardless of arguments or negative reinforcement from others. Values are applied appropriately when they are applied in the right area.

Personal values are implicitly related to choices. Values guide decisions by allowing for an individual's choices to be compared to each chosen associated values. Personal values established primary in life may be tough to modifications. Though, personal values are not universal in nature; yet they are determined by one's genes, family, nation and historical environment. This does not mean that the value notions themselves are not universal, simply that each individual hold an exclusive conception of them that is a peculiar information of the suitable values for their own genes, feelings and experience. Personal values are the beliefs, values, and philosophies that we possess about life, its perseverance, and our own purpose. While growing up, one take on board the personal values of others around us and start to accept or reject such values as being a part of which one is, or not a part of our own selves. It is easy, however, to pass by the active recognition and sorting of personal values, and to just accept those values that were deep-seated in us by parents, teachers, society, etc. Knowing the personal values of growing students will help the adults and teachers in the direction that they are moving and the type of guidance required for them. Proper counselling may be provided when students do not carry proper values and help them to acquire such values which help them to adjust in colleges, and prepare for future.

A value is a belief, a mission, or a philosophy that is meaningful. Whether we are consciously aware of them or not, every individual has a core set of personal values. Values can range from the commonplace, such as the belief in hard work and punctuality, to the more psychological, such as self-reliance, concern for others, and harmony of purpose. Value is a concept that describes the beliefs of an individual or culture. A set of values may be placed into the notion of a value system. Values are considered subjective and vary across people and cultures. Types of values include ethical/moral values, doctrinal/ideological (political, religious) values, social values, and aesthetic values. It is debated whether some values.

Personal values are principles that define you as an individual. Personal values, such as honesty, reliability, and trust, determine how you will face the world and relate with people. Personal values evolve from circumstances with the external world and can change over time. Integrity in the application of values refers to its continuity; persons have integrity if they apply their values appropriately regardless of arguments or negative reinforcement from others. Values are applied appropriately when they are applied in the right area. For example, it would be appropriate to apply religious values in times of happiness as well as in times of despair. Personal values are implicitly related to choice; they guide decisions by allowing for an individual's choices to be compared to each choice's associated values. Mashlah [1] found that there are robust links between people's personal values and the ways they think, feel, and act. The findings reflected how people's personal values drive, inspire, and lead them in making their decisions, building their perceptions, and shaping their attitudes and behaviour. On this basis of the study, researcher emphasized on the existing knowledge on the empirical impact of people's personal values on the way they think, feel, and act.

Values refer to what is good and worthy. They characterize both individuals and social Collectives, such as nations, business organizations, and religious groups. Values of social Collectives (often termed cultural values) represent the goals that members of the social Collective are encouraged to pursue, and they serve to justify actions taken by collective Members and leaders in pursuit of these goals Values of individuals (often termed personal Values) are broad desirable goals that motivate people's action and serve as guiding principles In their lives. They affect people's preferences and behavior over time and across Situations. In the current review article we focus on personal values.

Values are relatively stable and they tend to serve as consistent guiding systems for behavior. However, their functions can also be mildly modified depending on the context and perception of the current situation. This is crucial for hypothesizing that despite the observed value stability; values can also be used in a different manner by individuals with different needs and motivations. Consequently, it may be vital to distinguish the value–dishonesty analysis into low-achievers and high-achievers, who may be characterized by completely different motivations in their learning strategies. We therefore expect that some of the relationships of values with dishonest inclinations will be moderated by students' previous achievements (grades). High Security should be a negative predictor of academic dishonesty, especially among low-achievers – whose motivation to avoid future failures will be accompanied by their reluctance to engage in unsafe and risky behaviors. On the other hand, Self-Enhancement values (e.g., Achievement) should especially motivate high-achievers to avoid cheating and aim at mastery in terms of knowledge and competences.

1.5.1 Type of Values

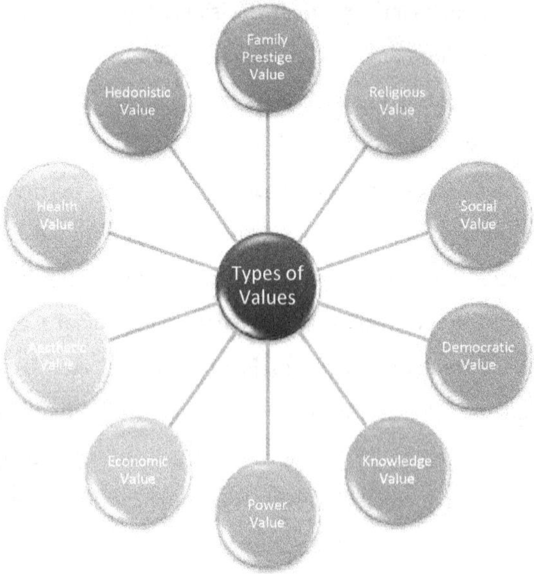

1. **Religious Value**

   This value is defined in terms of faith in God, attempt to understand him, fear of divine wrath and according to the ethical codes prescribed in the religious books, the outward acts of behaviour expressive of this value are going on pilgrimage, living a simple life, having faith in the religious leaders , worshipping God and speaking truth.

2. **Social Value**

   This value is defined in terms of charity , kindness , love and sympathy for the people efforts to serve God through the service of mankind, sacrificing personal comforts and gains to relieve the needy and the afflicted of their misery.

3. **Democratic Value**

   This value is characterized by respect for individuality, absence of discrimination among persons on the bases of sex, language, religion, caste, colour, race and family status, ensuring equal social, political and religious rights to all, impartially, social justice and respect for the democratic institutions.

4. **Aesthetic Value**

   Aesthetic Value is characterized by appreciation of beauty, form proportion and harmony, love for fine arts, drawing –painting, music, dance, sculpture, poetry and architecture, love for literature, love for decoration of home and the surroundings, neatness and system in the arrangement of the things.

5. **Economic Value**

   This value stands for desire for money and material gains. A man with high economic value is guided by considerations of money and material gain in the choice of his job. His attitude towards the rich persons and the industrialists is favourable and he considers them helpful for the progress of the country.

6. **Knowledge Value**

   This value stands for love of knowledge of theoretical principles of any activity, and love of discovery of truth. A man with knowledge value considers a knowledge of theoretical principles underlying a work essential for success in it. He values hard work in studies, only it helps develop ability to find out new facts and relationships and aspires to be known as the seeker of knowledge. For him knowledge is virtue.

7. **Hedonistic Value**

Hedonistic value is the conception of the desirability of living pleasure and avoiding pain. For a hedonist the present is more important than the future. A man with hedonist value indulges in pleasures of senses and avoids pain.

8. **Power Value**

Here the power value is defined as the conception of desirability of ruling over others and also of leading others. The characteristics of a person of high power value are that he prefers a job where he gets opportunity to exercise authority over others, that he prefers to rule in small place rather than serve in a big place, that fear of law of the country rather than the fear of God deters him from having recourse to unapproved means for making money, and that he is deeply status – conscious and can even tell a lie for maintaining the prestige of his position.

9. **Family Prestige Value**

As defined here, the family prestige value is the conception of the desirability of such items of behaviour, roles, functions and relationships as would become one's family status. It implies respect for roles which are traditionally characteristic of different castes of indian society . It also implies the maintenance on the purity of family blood by avoiding inter-caste marriages. It is respect for the conservative outlook as enshrined in the traditional institution of family.

10. **Health Value**

Health value is the consideration for keeping the body in a fit state for carrying out one's normal duties and functions. It also implies the consideration for self –preservation. A man with high health value really feels if through some act of negligence he impairs his health, he considers good physical health essential for the development and use of his abilities.

1.6. SUMMARY:

In the present study, the family environment, happiness and personal values of people were studied in relation to various variables such as relation to Type of family, Type of gender, Type of area

Whatever the type of research, It is very important to give a brief summary of the details presented in each chapter. So that anyone who studies the research report can get an idea of the research work

The study of reference literature is important in many ways in the social / behavioral sciences. Reference literature is useful in a number of ways in the research that will take place now. The next chapter is review of related literature. The next chapter deals with the study of family environment, happiness and personal values in different countries.

CHAPTER 2

REVIEW OF RELATED LITERATURE

2.1 Introduction & Importance of Literature Review

2.2 Review of Related Literatures for Family Environment

2.3 Review of Related Literatures for Happiness

2.4 Review of Related Literatures for Personal Values

2.5 Summary

2.1 INTRODUCTION & IMPORTANCE OF LITERATURE REVIEW:

Agrawal states that "A study of the relevant literature to define the problem And it is very necessary to builds its limits."

The rule of science is that from the subject matter which has been ploughed before new & new knowledge can be acquired. No research is done from scratch. But it only stems from research done in the past. Any Research derived from previous research to get something more innovative information from the principles or it may be for re-examination of the principles. Reading pre-research is necessary because the concept of the present research and other scholars were the clarity of the given concept so that the researcher idea about this becomes pure and firm so he can do research with more precision.

Previous research has been significant in many otherwise this will prevent the repetition of the same type of research. It can contain information about neglected variables. Also getting information about the schemes adopted by various practitioners the researcher can get good guidance on his research plan.

A study of previous research enthusiastic researcher to work on a new farm gives insight, skills and abilities. Researcher make scientific vision experimental. Pre exciting research helps in raising awareness about the importance and necessity of research work.

Day by day the horizons of education and research are wide open.it takes the form of a social process from individual. The study of previous research on the development of the individual and community helps to plan and build favourable conditions.

The study of the reference literature of research in the relevant field in the past is given to the researcher as follows is helpful.

(1) Useful in building a good hypothesis.

(2) Provides guidance on advanced method of research.

(3) Awakens insight into problem forms.

(4) Comparative study of matters related to the problem can be done.

The researcher realizes the different aspects of the chosen problem. Here we have tried to briefly review the research.

A literature review may consist of simply a summary of key sources, but in the social sciences, a literature review usually has an organizational pattern and combines both summary and synthesis, often within specific conceptual categories.

We also need a Literature Review for that, Compare and contrast each source to other relevant literature on the topic. Critically evaluate each source. Indicate how each source contributes to the body of knowledge about the topic. Integrate your discussion of the sources into your argument about the state of knowledge on the topic

2.2 REVIEW OF RELATED LITERATURES FOR FAMILY ENVIRONMENT:

Ashwini.P.Patil(2017) in their study titled **Examine the Role of Family Environment to the Development of Psychological Resilience among Urban and Rural Adolescents**

In this study examined the role of family environment to the development of psychological resilience among urban and rural adolescents. The sample consisted of 120 adolescents were selected for the study which includes 60 urban and 60 rural from Kolhapur districts. Random sampling method was used for the data collection. Resilience was measured by Adolescent Resilience Questionnaire (Deirdre Gartland, 2006) and family environment was measured by Family Environment Scale (Bhatia and Chadha, 1993). The Method of central tendency was used for data analysis and computes the Mean, SD and calculated ‘r’ and ‘t’ values. The results indicated that the there is a positive correlation between resilience and family environment among urban and rural adolescents. Whereas the mean score of rural adolescents is more than urban adolescent with respect to resilience and family environment, it’s showed that the level of resilience and family environment among rural living adolescents is higher than that of urban living adolescents. The findings also indicated that there is no significant difference found between resilience and family environment among urban and rural living adolescents.

Shanti Balda, Sheela Sangwan and Arti Kumari (2019)in their study titled **Family Environment as Perceived by Adolescent Boys and Girls.** The present study was conducted in Hisar city and two villages of Hisar district. Two Government Senior Secondary Schools (one for boys and one for girls) from rural area and two Government Senior Secondary Schools (one for boys and one for girls) from Hisar city were selected at random. The study was conducted with 16-18 years old adolescents. These adolescents were selected from randomly selected four Government Senior Secondary Schools. Total sample constituted of 240 adolescents, 120 from rural area and 120 from urban area. These 240 adolescents included 120 boys and 120 girls. Family environment was assessed with the help of Family Environment Scale (FES) by Bhatia and Chadha (2004). Fathers of majority of adolescents had education up to senior secondary level, while majority of mothers had education up to middle school level. Maximum number of adolescents belonged to lower income group followed by middle and high income groups. Adolescents were personally interviewed about their perception of family environment. Z-test was used to determine if there were statistically significant differences between family environment perceived by rural and urban adolescent boys and girls. Results revealed that urban adolescents perceived family environment as more cohesive, more expressive, more accepting and caring, and more independent as compared to rural adolescents. While, rural adolescents perceived family environment more organized than urban adolescents. Urban adolescents perceived family environment significantly much better than those from rural area. Adolescent boys perceived family environment as more expressive, more accepting and caring, more independent, while, adolescents girls perceived family environment as more organized and controlling. Adolescent boys perceived family environment significantly much better than adolescent girls.

Findings of the present study are useful for parents and caregivers of adolescents.

(Divya Raina and Dr.Geeta Balodi 2013) in their study titled **An Insight into the Family Environment of Indian Women in Relation to Female Foeticide and Girl Child.** The present study focuses on the Family Environment (FES) of married women in relation to their status and the cause behind female foeticide, conducted in the state of Uttarakhand, India. A total of 600 married women were taken, those with two male children (2Mc), those with one male and one female child(1Fc1Mc) and those with two female children(2Fc). The sample comprised of five blocks of Uttarakhand namely Doiwala, Raipur, Sahaspur, Kalsi and Vikas Nagar. The 't' test between 2Mc and 2Fc reveals the value as 7.29, between 2Fc and 1Fc1Mc as-4.86, and between 2Mc and 1Fc1Mc as 3.09, 'F' value shows that there exists a difference between the three groups f (2,585) = 34.37, difference between blocks is f(4.585) = 23.11, suggesting the existing difference in the family environment of these women. Various measures need to be taken to help women gain control over their lives by coming out of orthodox restrictions imposed undesirably on them.

Sushilkumar Maheshwari, Rintu Chaturvedi, Sandhya Gupta(2020)in their study titled **Impact Of Family Environment On Mental Wellbeing of Adolescent Girls: A Cross Sectional Survey.** The present study was aimed to assess the impact of family environment on the mental well-being of adolescent girls in selected villages of Western Punjab, India. **Materials and Methods:** Quantitative, descriptive, cross-sectional survey approach was used to assess the family environment and mental well-being of conveniently selected 900 adolescent girls (age of 11–19 years) in selected villages of Punjab using sociodemographic data sheet, Family Environment Scale and Warwick Edinburgh mental well-being scale. **Results:** Approximately two-third (36.7%) of the adolescent's girls have below-average mental well-being, whereas the majority (62.2%) of adolescent girls have average, and only 1.1% have above-average mental well-being.

Mental well-being was positively correlated with cohesion, acceptance, and caring at $P < 0.01$ level, and expressiveness, independence, active recreational orientation, and organization were positively correlated at $P < 0.05$ level. Conflict and control were not significantly correlated with mental well-being. **Conclusion:** It can be concluded that there was a significant positive relationship between various domains of family environment with mental well-being among adolescent girls. Mental health professionals and community health nurses should take the early initiative to identify any malfunction in families to avoid possible deterioration in mental well-being and psychological problems among adolescent girls.

Santawana.G.Mishra(2019)in their study titled **Gender Wise study of Family Climate For Adolescents in Urban India .** The present research work is aimed to study the family climate of adolescents from urban families in association with their gender. A total of 309 adolescents (163 boys and 146 girls) in the age group of 14–15 years were randomly selected from the secondary schools of Aurangabad, a city in Maharashtra state of India for the academic year 2016–2017. The tool used for data collection was family climate scale (FCS) developed by Dr Beena Shah and published by National Psychological Corporation, Agra, India. In this test, family climate means an interpersonal relationship between the parents and the child. The test assesses the family climate on 10 dimensions. Data were collected by personally meeting the adolescents. The collected data were analyzed using chi-squared test. The study showed that more male adolescents had favorable family climate as compared to female adolescents and the difference was significant. Also, the number of female adolescents having unfavorable family climate was significantly higher as compared to male adolescents. The study concluded that the age-old gender bias is still very much prevalent in India. The boys are favoured and given a more conducive and positive family atmosphere as compared to the girls. Hence, there is a need for creating awareness to curb this bias and help the girls in the family to be treated at par with their male counterparts.

Kiran sahu, Dheerja Shah(2014)in their study titled **A Study Of Family Environment And Adjustment Of Young Adults.** The aim of the present study is to find out the relationship between family environment and adjustment among young adults and further to find out the gender differences regarding these variables. For this purpose 100 young adults(50 male and 50 female)were taken &Moradabad District of U.P. Family Relationship Scale(FES)(1993) by Bhatia and Chadha and Adjustment Inventory by Sinha and Singh were used for measuring family environment and adjustment of these young adults respectively. Results indicated that these young adults have good level of adjustment as well as family environment. In addition, males and females were significantly differed on these variables and some of its dimensions. Further, correlational analysis elucidated that there was positive correlation between family environment and adjustment. This implies that if the environment of family is good and motivating and cohesiveness is found among family members, the adjustment capacity of these young adults will increased and resulted in happy and healthy personality.

Dr Manoranjan Tripathy, Bisweswari Sahu(2019)in their study titled **Impact of Family Environment On Socio-Emotional Adjustment of Adolescent Girls In Rural Areas Of Western Odisha.** The purpose of the study was to assess the effect of the adolescent girls' family environment and their socio-emotional adjustment. A sample of study was included in one hundred teenagers of the age group between 17-18 years. Family Environment Scale (FES) and Adjustment Inventory for School Students (AISS) were administered. Data was analyzed in terms of percentage and multiple regression analysis. The statistical analysis revealed that all the eight family environment factors, viz. cohesion, expressiveness conflict, acceptance and caring, independence, active-recreational orientation, organization and control together showed significant role in socio-emotional and educational adjustment of adolescent girls. Based on the findings, it was recommended among others that families should reduce conflict and increase cohesion as this may have positive effect on the psychological adjustment of the adolescents.

Ms. Goldy Gupta(2017)in their study titled **A Comparative Study Of Family Environment Of Working Women of Government and private Sector.** The present research endeavor aimed to do comparative study of family environment of working women of government and private sector. The sample of the study consisted of 400 working women from Churu and Jaipur district of Rajasthan state. Out of which 200 were working in private sector and other 200 were from government sector. Family Environment Scale was used for the collection of data. Mean, S.D. and t-test were used for the analysis of data. The results indicated that there is significant difference exists between family environment of working women of private and government sector.

Mary Antony P, Manikandan.K(2015) in their study titled **Roll of Self Efficiency and Family Environment in Regulating Psychological Wellbeing Of Adolescents.**The aim of the study was to understand the role of self-efficacy and family interactions and environment in regulating psychological wellbeing of adolescents. Self-efficacy is the beliefs that individuals hold about their own abilities to make plans for and execute tasks within a specific domain to effectively lead to specific goals. Family plays vital role in moulding individuals' personality. Family environment characterized by conflict, unhealthy relationships and poor parenting are closely associated with building up troublesome individuals. Psychological well-being is usually conceptualized as some combination of positive affective states such as happiness and functioning with optimal effectiveness in individual and social life. Adolescents have very special and distinct needs and be treated carefully which in turn helps in developing robust citizens for the country. The participants of the study consist of 200 adolescents and collected data using Self-efficacy Scale, Family Environment Scale, Psychological Well Being Scale and Personal Information sheet. Results revealed that there exist significant sex difference among adolescents in variables such as psychological wellbeing and sub dimensions of family environment organization and control. There exists significant religious difference for variables self-efficacy, psychological wellbeing and two dimensions of family environment namely intellectual cultural orientation and moral religious emphasis. In the case of family type neither nuclear nor joint have any significant difference between self-efficacy, psychological wellbeing and also on ten dimensions of family environment.

Varma & Dhawan (2006) in their study titled **Psychological factors and mental health of contemporary Indian women.** conducted a study on 195 young urban educated married women with age range from 25-35 years. The results indicated that Indian women exhibited high level of well-being. The dimension of family group support contributed more to well-being. It was also found that women were able to control their major domains of lives and used active coping strategies to better their sense of well-being.

Sidrah Jamal , Mrs. Sandhya Bhatt(2020) in their study titled **Family environment and Adjustment among Young Adults.**The purpose of this paper is to investigate the association between family environment and adjustment. The research was conducted on a sample of individuals belonging to the age group of 18 to 21 years. The tools used for the research were family environment scale by Bhatia and Chadha and Bell Adjustment inventory (adult form). The results of this study have showed that all the dimensions of family environment scale are i.e. cohesion, expressiveness, conflict, acceptance, independence, active-recreational orientation, organization and control are positively correlated with home, health, emotional and social adjustment. In conclusion it has been seen that family environment has an impact on adjustment of an individual.

V. Ramaprabou(2014) in their study titled **The effect of family environment on the adjustment patterns of adolescents.** The present investigation was undertaken to study the effect of family environment on adjustment patterns. For this70 adolescents studying undergraduate programmes were randomly selected from the Arts and Science Colleges of Puducherry. Family Environment Scale by Harpreet and Chadha (1993) and Adjustment Inventory for College students constructed and standardized by Sinha and Singh(1971)was used for data collection .Analysis was done by using one way ANOVA. Findings of the study revealed that family environment has significant effect on the adjustment patterns of the students.

Deepshikha and Suman Bhanot(2011) in their study titled **Role of Family Environment on Socio-emotional Adjustment of Adolescent Girls in Rural Areas of Eastern Uttar Pradesh** The present study was conducted at Kumarganj, Faizabad District of Eastern Uttar Pradesh. The purpose of the study was to assess family environment of adolescent girls and its impact on their socio-emotional adjustment. One hundred adolescent girls of age group between 17-18 years comprised the sample of the study. Family Environment Scale (FES) and Adjustment Inventory for School Students (AISS) were administered. Data was analyzed in terms of percentage and multiple regression analysis. The statistical analysis revealed that all the eight family environment factors, viz. cohesion, expressiveness conflict, acceptance and caring, independence, active-recreational orientation, organization and control together showed significant role in socio-emotional and educational adjustment of adolescent girls.

2.3 REVIEW OF RELATED LITERATURES FOR HAPPINESS:

Doshi Dhara , Yogesh jogasan(2013)in their study titled **Depression And Psychological Well-Being in Old Age.**The main purpose of this research was to find out the mean difference between adult and aged in depression and psychological well being. The total 60 sample were taken out which 30 were adult (20 to 59 years) male and female and 30 were aged (60 years and above) male and female. The research tool for depression, Beck depression inventory was used. Here Guajarati adaption used. For psychological well being, Sudha Bhogle's Psychological well being scale was used, translated in Gujarati and the t-test was applied to check the difference of depression and psychological well being and the Karl-person 'r' method used to check the correlation. Result reveals that significant difference in depression and psychological well being with respect to both adult and aged. While co-relation between depression and psychological well-being reveals -0.70 negative correlation.

Bidisha Chakraborty, Souparna Maji, Anamika Sen, Isha Malik , Sayantan Baidya, Esha Dwibedi(2018)in their study titled **A Study On Happiness And Related Factors Among Indian College Students.**This paper studies the happiness of Indian college and university students aged between 18 and 24 years. It attempts to answer whether and to what extent happiness of a student is significantly related to aspects of social life such as time spent with family, friends, being in a relationship, logging into social networking sites; academic factors such as job prospects of the chosen field of study and academic environment; and other personal factors such as health condition, over thinking or dwelling on past bad memories, addiction to tobacco/drug/alcohol. Moreover, this paper also inquires about the relationship between a student's average happiness with her gender as well as the income class to which she belongs. It has been observed that among different aspects of social life, time spent with family and friends are significant while logging into social networking site is found out to be insignificant. Also being in a relationship is significantly but negatively related to happiness for male students. Job Prospects of the current field of study is a highly significant covariate of happiness irrespective of the gender of the student. Among different aspects of the personal situation, dwelling on past bad memories decreases happiness of both male and female students. Addiction to tobacco/alcohol is a negative covariate of female happiness. Furthermore, income and gender are seen to play an insignificant role in the happiness of Indian college and university students.

Zi –qing Yuan , Xian Zheng, Eddie C.M.Hui(2020)in their study titled **Happiness Under One Roof? The Intergenerational Co-residence and subjective well-being of Elders in china** This study investigates the relationship between intergenerational co-residence and the subjective well-being (SWB) of elders based on the individual-level panel data collected from the Chinese Longitudinal Healthy Longevity Survey from 2002 to 2014. They used the endogenous treatment effect model to minimize selection bias and estimate the causal impacts of intergenerational co-residence on parental SWB.

In addition, they employ the individual fixed-effect model for robustness checks. Results corroborate that elders who live with their adult–children are happier than those who do not undergo such a living arrangement. They also investigate heterogeneous effects across geographical regions and demographic groups. Older people in rural areas who co-reside with their adult–children gain a more substantial co-residence effect compared with those in urban areas. Moreover, results are robust according to different specifications. Their findings provide useful implications for policymakers in promoting the SWB of elders.

Hasida Ben – Zur (2003)in their study titled **Happy Adolescents : The Link between Subjective Wellbeing , Internal Resources and parental Factors.** The research investigates the associations of personal and parental factors with subjective well-being (SWB) in adolescents on the basis of 2 studies. The first included 97 university students and 185 adolescents who completed questionnaires measuring perceived mastery, dispositional optimism, and affect used as a measure of SWB. Correlations and hierarchical regression analyses showed mastery and optimism to be negatively associated with negative affect (NA) and positively associated with positive affect (PA). Demographic variables did not relate to PA and NA except for gender, with female adolescents showing higher levels of NA than males. The second study included 121 adolescents and their parents who completed questionnaires measuring mastery, optimism, SWB indicators, and assessments by the adolescents of their relationships with their parents. The associations of the adolescents' mastery and optimism with SWB measures were positive and were similar to those found in the first study. Positive correlations were found between the adolescents' and their parents' SWB (especially with their father's), but no significant associations were observed between adolescents' and parents' mastery and optimism. However, adolescents' mastery and optimism were related to positive relationships with parents. The results highlight the importance of mastery, optimism, and positive adolescent–parent relationships in contributing to the well-being of adolescents.

Sudeshna Ghosh , Subrata Lahiri, Nitin Datta(2017) in their study titled **Understanding Happiness And Psychological Well-Being Among Young Married Women In Rural India**The paper examines happiness and psychological well-being and its influence by various aspects of marriage among young married women. Multistage sampling technique was used to interview 654 married women, 13-24 years in rural West Bengal. Mean age at marriage was found to be 16 years. One-third reported adjustment problem initially after marriage. Logistic regression analysis results showed marital happiness was positively influenced by less spousal difference in opinion; couple educational status, able to adjust marital problems and wish to have same life partner given an option of partner selection. No significant association was found between happiness and type of marriage and husband's currently staying with wife.

Dr Chythra R. Rao(2017) in their study titled **Are Rural Adults Happy ? An Observational Study of Happiness And Its Determinants.** The study was designed to assess happiness among rural adults and to identify various socio- demographic, family and health determinants affecting happiness.

Methods: It was a cross sectional study conducted in the field practice area of Department of Community Medicine, KMC Manipal. The study included 403 permanent residents of field practice area, aged ≥20 years, of both gender and willing to participate in the study. Information pertaining to socio-demographic characteristics, details pertaining to co-morbidities, habits and family particulars were collected by personal interviews using a pre-designed questionnaire. Happiness was assessed using the Oxford happiness questionnaire.

Results: A total of 403 subjects participated in the study and among them 82% of the respondents were happy and 17.6% were unhappy, as per the Oxford happiness questionnaire. Over half of the participants belonged to 30-60 years and two-thirds were females (66.5%). There was no gender difference in reported happiness. Almost all the people who had cordial relationship with family members (99.1%) and neighbor- hood (97.9%), owning a house (94%) and being without co-morbidities (56%) were happy. Past hospitalization, concerns about child marriage and employment made people less happy.

Conclusions: Good relationship with family members and neighbor-hood, absence of co-morbidities was positive determinants of happiness, while hospitalization, concerns about employment and marriage of their children contributed to unhappiness.

Kamlesh kumar Patel, MurliDhar(2018) in their study titled **Marital Happiness Among Newly Married Individuals in Rural District in India.** The present study was conducted to assess the level of happiness and its associated factors in a rural population in India. Primary data was collected from a cross-sectional survey of newly married (for at least one year but not more than five years) individuals (N=256, male: 136 and female: 120) in rural Varanasi district in Uttar Pradesh. Multistage PPS sampling was applied to select the study subjects. The measurement of marital happiness was based on standard and widely verified marital happiness scale. In addition, marital happiness as perceived by the individuals was also assessed. Level of happiness was assessed descriptively and ordered logistic regression was applied to examine the factors. Important significantly associated factors contributing to the lack of happiness were social support (positively), wealth (poor happier), marital duration (negatively), age (23-26 age-group happier), family type (nuclear family happier) and sex (men happier). Social-support may play a key role in the formulation of policies. In addition, the findings may provide useful clues to the social workers and counsellors associated with marital well-being.

Sharma Shailendra kumar, Srivastava. S.K(2013) in their study titled **Happiness and Unhappiness in Rural Areas : Meaning , Causes and Variations.** The Objective of the study was understand the meaning , causes , variation and coping strategies of Happiness and Unhappiness. Data was collected using scales, interviews and observation in rural areas on 50 head of the families. The respondents mostly belonged to OBC caste category and family structure varied from nuclear, lineal and joint to collateral families. Data was analyzed manually and chi squares, net balances and cross tabulations were done. Findings of the study reveal that most respondents are Unhappy in their life because their net balances are negative. Respondents have experienced achievement, life cycle events, social support and spiritual events as a source of happiness. These events promote their sustainability of livelihood. The source of unhappiness are emphasized in terms of loss of life , loss of crop productivity , failure in life, loss of property , breach of trust and breakdown of social cohesion.

Komal Vyas (2020)in their study titled **A Study Of The Happiness Among The Students With ReferenceTo Their Education Level And Gender.**The present study is of Happiness among students pursuing graduation and post-graduation studies. This study is aimed to check happiness with reference to types of level of education and gender. The happiness scale (RHMJ) prepared by Dr.Himanshi Rastogi and Dr.Janki Moorjani (2017) was used. The sample constituted total 120 students out of which 60 are from graduation (30 boys and 30 girls) and 60 are from post-graduation (30 boys and 30 girls).The data was collected from various colleges of Ahmedabad city of Gujarat state. The data was scored and analyzed as per the norms of manual. 'F'-test was being calculated for this study. Then the result of study showed that (1) There is significant difference between the mean score of the happiness among boys and girls students. So it could be said that the boys group is having more happiness than girl group. (2)There is significant difference between the mean score of the happiness among study in graduation and post-graduation students.so it could be said that study in graduation students group is having more happiness than study in post-graduation students group. (3) There is no significant difference between interactive effect of the mean of the mean score of the happiness among gender and level of education.

Komal Vyas (2021)in their study titled **A Study Of The Happiness Among The People With Reference To Their Marital Status And Gender.** The present study is of Happiness among people who have status with married and unmarried. This study is aimed to check happiness with reference to types of marital status and gender. The happiness scale (RHMJ) prepared by Dr.Himanshi Rastogi and Dr.Janki Moorjani (2017) was used. The sample constituted total 120 people out of which 60 are from married (30 male and 30 female) and 60 are unmarried (30 male and 30 female).The data was collected from various areas of Ahmedabad city of Gujarat state. The data was scored and analyzed as per the norms of manual. 'F'- test was being calculated for this study. Then the result of study showed that (1) There is significant difference between the mean score of the happiness among male and female. So it could be said that the male group is having more happiness than female group. (2)There is significant difference between the mean score of the happiness among married people and unmarried people .so it could be said that married people group is having more happiness than unmarried people group. (3) There is no significant difference between interactive effect of the mean score of the happiness among gender and marital status.

Dinesh singh , Amita Malik(2012) in their study titled **spirituality and Happiness: A correlated study** The present study was designed to assess and compare the level of spirituality and happiness of males and females of different rural and urban areas of District Rohtak and explore the relationship the correlation between spirituality and happiness. A2x2 factorial design was adopted for the present study. The study was conducted over a sample of 200 (100 males and 100 females) of the age group of 20-40 years. Out of them 100 subjects (50 males and 50 females) were selected from different rural areas and 100 subjects (50 males and 50 females) were selected from different urban areas on random basis. Structured Interview Schedule was used to assess the level of spirituality. Revised Oxford Happiness Scale was used to assess the level of happiness of the subjects. It was hypothesized that there will be a significant difference between rural and urban as well as male and female in the level of spirituality and happiness. It was also hypothesized that there will be a significant positive relationship between spirituality and happiness of the subjects. The obtained data was analysed by mean, SD, t-test and Pearson 'r'. No significant difference was found in level of spirituality as well as happiness due to differences of sex and residential background of the subjects. A significant moderate positive relationship was found between the level of spirituality and happiness of the subjects. On the basis of the finding of the study it may be concluded that spiritual and religious belief serves as source of attachment, security and confidence and motivate people to strive for their life goals and live happily.

Carol Graham; Soumya Chattopadhyay (2013) in their study titled **Gender and Well-being around the world.** They explore gender differences in reported well-being around the world, both across and within countries - comparing age, income, and education cohorts. They find that women have higher levels of well-being than men, with a few exceptions in low income countries. They also find differences in the standard relationships between key variables - such as marriage and well-being - when differential gender rights are accounted for. They conclude that differences in well-being across genders are affected by the same empirical and methodological factors that drive the paradoxes underlying income and well-being debates, with norms and expectations playing an important mediating role.

Maurizio Pugno (2015) in their study titled **Trust, family and education.** The capacity to enhance people's general trust, which is proved to be important for economic growth and individual well-being, is usually attributed to the family and education. This paper first draws attention to two awkward facts: that placing a great deal of importance on family ties has detrimental effects on general trust (although it brings well-being); and that education tends to be designed to enhance competition rather than cooperation. The paper then proposes people's 'social skill' as the target variable for research and policy, since it is both proximate to general trust and can be learned as an enjoyable experience, especially, but not only, in the first part of people's lives. The family and education should be thus orientated according to this new specific perspective.

Elizabeth Terrazas-Carrillo; Paula T. McWhirter; Hannah K. Muetzelfeld (2016) in their study titled **Happy parents in latin America?**

Exploring the impact of gender, work- family satisfaction, and parenthood on general life happiness. This study explores the impact of gender, employment, parenthood, and work-family satisfaction on happiness in three Latin American countries using data from the 2002 International Social Survey. Results indicated the existence of significant differences in happiness, family life satisfaction, and division of household labour between Latin American men and women who report being married and working full-time. Overall, men were happier than women but women experienced higher levels of family life satisfaction. Results from a regression analysis indicate being male, having high levels of job and family satisfaction, and presence of children in the household are positive predictors of happiness. However, being female and experiencing time binds have a negative impact on general life happiness. Contrary to research in Western countries, children were found to be a source of increased happiness for employed and married Latin American men and women. Results are discussed in the context of cultural differences in gender and marriage values.

Donghwan Kim (2018) in their study titled **The effect of urbanisation level and mobility on happiness in OECD countries.** This article examines the effects of urbanisation level and mobility on happiness in organisation for economic cooperation and development (OECD) countries using data provided by World Bank and OECD statistics. Although the focus on the relationship between urbanisation and happiness has been growing, the researchers have not been able adequately to define an urban or rural class due to the complex characteristics of a cross-national analysis. The link between mobility and happiness has not been studied extensively, and the relationship between mobility and happiness has not been proven consistently. The data in this study were calculated and compiled with relatively homogeneous and consistent criteria. This article concluded that the urbanisation level and mobility have a negative relationship with happiness. In addition, it identified different geographical patterns of happiness. Eastern Asian countries are characterised by high levels of urbanisation compared to other countries. Northern and

Western European countries were happier compared to other countries with similar levels of economic developments. Eastern and Southern European countries were unhappier, even though their urbanisation levels are like those in Northern and Western European countries. The results obtained in this paper could help create public policies to enhance happiness.

Kenneth M. Cramer; Rebecca Pschibul (2019) in their study titled **Finding skeleton key to happiness : evaluating model invariance of subjective well-being in comparison of large urban centres world wide.**The present study compared the antecedents that contribute to personal happiness from several large urban centres around the world, testing the hypothesis of model invariance that supposes any given model may be applied globally. Data from an archival dataset (Lee, 2006) included various elements of city life: economy, culture and education, income, safety, living conditions, city administration, health, city pride, and current level of happiness. Results showed each urban centre required a unique profile of antecedents, offering little evidence to support the invariance assumption. Overall, health was the most common predictor of happiness (especially for males), followed by city pride and household income. Lower explained variance was typical among the samples, suggesting that additional factors are required to capture the scope of urban quality of life. Future research directions are discussed.

Helmut Warmenhoven; Paul R.J. Hoebink; Jan M.A.M. Janssens (2019) in their study titled **Subjective well-being of the Chinese post-reform generation: influence of family income and urban/rural origin on the happiness of Chinese students.** This paper reports on a study among 711 Chinese students from the post-reform generation, comparing the subjective wellbeing of urban and rural students from different family income groups, using the Personal Wellbeing Index of the International Wellbeing Group. Urban participants were found to be more satisfied with their standard of living and their life-achievements than their rural counterparts, but no differences were found between these two groups for happiness, overall satisfaction with life, and the other five Personal Wellbeing Index satisfaction domains. In terms of family income level, participants from higher income families were found to be happier than participants from lower income families, and they were significantly more satisfied with their life (overall), as well as with their standard of living, life-achievement, personal relationships, feeling part of the community, and future (financial) security.

Pankhuri Aggarwal, Vaishali.V.Raval, Anuradha sathiyaseelan, Mackenzie trevethan, Aaron.M.Luebbe in their study titled Scripts About Happiness Among Urban Families in South India. The ways in which parents socialize positive emotions have important implications for youth wellbeing, though little is known about parental goals and responses to adolescents' happiness in culturally diverse families. Using an open-ended qualitative methodology, we explored parent and adolescent views about situations leading to happiness, responses and justifications to the expression of happiness, and what parents would like to teach their children about happiness in a sample of 209 parent (56.3% fathers; *M*age = 42.79 years) and adolescent (85.2% girls, *M*age = 14.95 years) dyads in Bengaluru, India. When prompted to identify adolescents' recent experiences of happiness, both parents and adolescents primarily described academic and extracurricular achievements, followed by special events and receipt of tangible items, social interactions, and overcoming difficult situations. The two most common parent responses to adolescents' happiness were responding with appreciation or encouragement of the achievement and providing further instruction or advice, with fewer responses focusing on enhancing/maintaining the emotional state of happiness itself. A substantial proportion of participating parents reported that their child should focus on task improvement when feeling happy, followed by affect maintenance (i.e., the child should "be happy"), or express their emotion with restraint. The findings contribute to developing a culturally-informed understanding of socialization of happiness in diverse families.

2.4 REVIEW OF RELATED LITERATURES FOR PERSONAL VALUES:

Mayurakshee Gangopadhyay, Dr Debomita Sikdar(2016) in their study titled **Effect of Personal values on Psychological well-being of Urban and Rural Youth.** The aim of the present study is to find out the effect of personal values on psychological well-being of urban and rural youth. To serve this objective a sample of 600 youth were selected by stratified random sampling. They were college students aged between 18-21 years. The data was collected from Kolkata and its adjacent areas. A general information schedule, Personal Values Questionnaire by Sherry and Verma (1978) and Psychological Well-Being Scale by Sisodia and Choudhary (2005) were administered on the samples. The findings revealed that the means of dimensions of values like democratic, aesthetic, economic, knowledge, hedonistic and power value and dimensions of psychological well- being like satisfaction, efficiency, sociability, mental health, interpersonal relations and over all psychological wellbeing are higher in case of urban youth than rural youth. And for other dimensions of values like religious, social, family prestige and health value the mean values of rural youth are higher than that of the urban youth. But rural youth are not higher in any dimension of psychological well-being than the urban youth. It also showed that there is significant difference between rural and urban youth in terms of values and psychological well-being. There exists significant impact of values on psychological wellbeing of youth. Life satisfactions, efficiency, sociability, mental health, inter personal relations etc. are major components of a person's psychological well-being that get shaped or influenced by the value system being it an important socio-cultural component.

Anand ,Himani, Pratap, Shailendra , Guatami,S.(2012) in their study titled **Effect of Religious Values On Life Satisfaction .** This studies have identified several variables that influence the level of life satisfaction. Variables such as health, age, gender impact the life satisfaction. Aim: To study the effect of religious values on life satisfaction. Materials and Methods:

The sample consisted of a total of 60 adolescents (30 boys and 30 girls) of age between 18 and 22 years. Personal Value Questionnaire (PVQ) developed by G. P. Sherry and R. P. Verma and Life Satisfaction Scale (LSS) developed by Q.G. Alam, and Ramji Srivastava were administered to measure religious values and life satisfaction. Chi-square was used to find the effect of religious values on life satisfaction. Findings and Conclusions: The findings of the study show that religious values gives positive thoughts conducts and actions so that a man can develop himself with all dimensions of life successfully and become a satisfied person.

Himani Anand, Shailendra Pratap(2012) in their study titled **Effect of Knowledge Values on Life Satisfaction Among Adolescents.** The present study was designed to study the effect of knowledge values on life satisfaction. The sample consisted of 60 adolescents in the age range of 15 to 24 years. Life satisfaction and Personal Values were measured by Life Satisfaction Scale prepared by Q.G. Alam and Ramji Srivastava and Personal Values Questionnaire (PVQ) prepared by G. P. Sherry and R.P. Verma respectively. x2 was applied to study the effect of knowledge values on life satisfaction. Results indicated that there is a significant relationship between knowledge values and life satisfaction. Person with knowledge values works hard for develop his knowledge and ability. For him knowledge is virtue. It is clear that values gives positive thoughts, conducts and actions so that a man can develop himself with all dimensions of life successfully and become a satisfied person.

Chacko Nisha , Mathur Anjali , Shiekh Sarita (2019) in their study titled **Values of Adolescents As Impacted By Gender.** The present study was an attempt to find out the impact of gender on the value system for adolescents for which a total of 300 samples comprising of 150 adolescent boys and the same number of girls in the age group of 12-18 years were selected using stratified random sampling technique from various Schools and Colleges of Allahabad District. The data was obtained using standardized tests like revised Socio Economic Status Scale by (Kumar and Tiwari, 2012) and Personal Value Questionnaire devised by (Sherry and Verma, 1998). The results revealed a highly significant difference among boys and girls regarding their religious values, aesthetic values and family prestige value wherein girls had higher religious values, aesthetic value and family prestige values as compared to the boys. A highly significant difference in the power values of boys and girls was also seen wherein the power values of boys were higher than the power values of girls. A non-significant gender variation was found regarding the social values, democratic values, economic values, knowledge values, hedonistic values, health values and total personal values of adolescents.

Pavithra N, Abha Ahuja, Ritu Singh(2020) in their study titled **A comparative Study on The Personal Values of Male Adolescents Across Different Group With Respect to Their Family Income.** Aim of the present study was conducted to assess and compare the personal values among male adolescents in the families categorized under three group based on their family income as Low Level Income Group (LLIG), Medium-Level Income Group (MLIG) and High-Level Income Group (HLIG). The total sample consisted of 90 male adolescents in the age group of 17-19 years from the two selected colleges of GB Pant University of Agriculture and Technology (College of Home Science and College of Agriculture), Pantnagar. From the selected colleges, the students were randomly drawn under three classified groups within the age group irrespective of their degree program. The list of male students enrolled in I and II year (of both Agriculture and Home Science within the age group of 17-19 years) made was collected from the office of four colleges and scrutinized under three groups based on their family income. The sample of 30 male adolescent students was randomly selected under each group constituting the total sample of 90students. The Deans of both the colleges were personally contacted for seeking permission to have rapport and collect the information legally. Self-structured general information questionnaire along with the Personal value questionnaire by Sherry and Verma [8] was administered to collect the data. **Results**: The results revealed that the family income plays a crucial role in the personal values of adolescents. Except for social and religious values, the students from HLIG are having a significantly high level of personal values when compared to LLIG and MLIG. Hence, the higher the family income, the more focus on personal development and so the improved personal values of the younger generations.

Ishina Bagga, Sarita Saini(2017) in their study titled **A comparative Analysis Of the Value System of Adolescent and their Parents.**The present research was taken up to investigate and analyze the differences in the value system of adolescents and their parents. The sample for the study comprised of 100 school going adolescents (boys=50&girls=50) in the age group of 16 to 18 years of age and their parents (fathers=100&mothers=100) selected from two schools of Ludhiana city, during the session 2015-2016.The value system of adolescents and their parents was assessed by using Personal Values Questionnaire (PVQ) developed by Sherry and Verma (1971). The analysis of the data revealed that parents valued religion and health more than their children, whereas, adolescents surpassed their parents in economic and hedonistic values. Daughters were found to be more appreciative of aesthetics and sons were found to be more power oriented than their mothers. However, mothers had higher aesthetic value than fathers.

Mohammad Hassan Asayesh, Hamid bahramizadeh(2011) in their study titled **Examination Of Personal Values System And Its Changes Among Young People.** The main purpose of this study was investigated youth values system and it's changing in male and female to answer this question whether a change in values has been created. The results of this study are compared with previous studies. Eighty-seven (33 male, 54 female) students from Semnan University in Iran were participated in this study. All participants completed the Personal Values Questionnaire (PVQ). The results showed that there is no significant difference between male and female in Religious, social, Public, Aesthetic, Economic, Knowledge, Hedonism, Power, Health values. Compared with the previous studies these findings showed that male and female has changed. In comparison to the previous findings, these findings show that the male and female's values have undergone some changes. But there is a significant difference between the two genders regarding value of family face. These findings work as warring toward the reduction of families' power in transferring the appropriate values to each gender. Finally, regarding the key role of family in transferring the values to their children, it is suggested that parents consult with the experts for having a mental and emotional communication with their children and internalization cultural values in them.

Sanjay K Das, Shobha Gupta , Madhuri Datta(2016) in their study titled **Comparison PVQ between Extrovert Rural And Urban Females.** The objective of the present study was to compare the personal values between extrovert rural and extrovert urban females. PVQ is taken as a set of dependent variable whereas extrovert traits of personality and rural and urban fields are taken as set of independent variables. It was hypothesized that females of urban and rural area will differ on their mean for value pattern. This assumption is based on findings of Bhatia et al. (2007) and Devi and Vig . (2014). A sample of 360 females from urban area and similar number from rural area were selected with the help of random sampling technique. Results indicate that urban females (extrovert) do not believe in social inequality, however, rural adolescents gave more value to family prestige than urban adolescents. Rural adolescents believed in maintenance of purity of family blood by avoiding inter-caste marriages.

Jagminder kaur, Harpreet kaur (2013) in their study titled **personal values of college girls in relation to type of college and educational level of their mothers.**The main objective of the study was to compare the personal values of girls in relation to type of college and educational level of their mothers. The study was delimited to 216 college girls out of which 108 was from the private colleges and 108 was from government colleges of Ludhiana and Sangrur districts only. Personal Value Questionnaire (PVQ) by Dr. G.P. Sherry and R.P. Verma and an Information sheet prepared by the investigator has been used to assess the variable and sub-variables of the study. Mean scores, Standard deviation and t-ratio revealed that i) A significant difference exists between social value of girls studying in private and government colleges, ii) A significant difference exists between family prestige value of college girls of under-graduate and graduate mothers. Iii) A significant difference exists between aesthetic value of college girls of under-graduate and post-graduate mothers. Iv) A significant difference exists between hedonistic value of college girls of graduate and post-graduate mothers.

Dr. Sachin Kaushik (2016) in their study Titled **A Study of Values Among Female Adolescents in Relation to Their Locality at Senior Secondary Level** The study was undertaken with the purpose of studying values of female adolescent in relation to their locality. This study was conducted on a sample of 150 female adolescents 75 rural female and 75 urban female studying in senior secondary school at Meerut District. Value test developed by G.P. Sherry was used. Indian adaptation of values inventory were administered on the students. Result confirmed that there was an significant different between the rural female adolescents and urban female adolescents in regards to their Social, Knowledge, Aesthetic, Power, Family and Health values. Also the urban and rural female adolescents differ significantly in relation to their Religious, Democratic, Economic and Hedonistic values.

Goldy Gupta (2016) in their study titled **A Comparative Study of Personal Values of Male and Female Secondary Teachers of Rewari District**. Value makes life worthwhile, education enriches it and society provides circumstances in which one could lead it successfully or whatever it may mean from time to time. Whole educational system revolves around the teachers. Teachers occupy the pivot role. He is at the core of the process who can 'mend or end' the future of the individual, society and nation. But the teachers' thinking, feeling and actions are guided by his personal values. It is a matter of great sorrow that today secondary teachers have proved themselves worthless to great extent. They have not been justifying themselves as they thought to have their educational growth, standard, ideology and other aspects of their personality are embarrassing to the society. What is the mirror of their value pattern, how it can be modified; for it, the researcher took a sample of

100 secondary teachers; out of which 50 male and 50 female secondary teachers. After collecting and analyzing data, it was found that there is significant difference between the personal values of male and female secondary teachers at religious value, social value, democratic value, hedonistic and power value.

Pinto Arthur Charles , Dr. Jigar Parikh (2017) in their study titled **Influence of Gender on the Personal Values of Higher Secondary Students.** Values play an important role in successful living. The presences of one's values are reflected in the way one behaves talks and perceives things. It helps a person essentially to achieve the academic and professional excellence which will in return make them a good citizen of the country. To build a bright future, one must start the process from an early age itself. It is accepted fact that the values learned in childhood remain forever. It is not only helps one to distinguish from good and evil but also helps one to handle difficult situations easily and systematically. Therefore people with good values and ethics are given preference everywhere and are admired for their nature. The aim of present research is to find out the differences in personal values among boys and girls studying in Higher Secondary level. The researcher has used Personal Values Questionnaire (PVQ-SV) by Sherry G.P. and Verma R.P. as a tool. The present study was confined to 120 higher secondary students from Ahmedabad city. Even though, many factors influence personal values of an individual, the present study measures the values with regard to gender with ten different factors. After the analysis of the data, independent 't' test was applied to check significance. The finding reveals significant difference in economic value, power value and health value with regard to gender. The girls desire more economic value whereas the boys choose power value and health value.

Yumkhaibam anandi Devi and Deepikavig (2014) in their study titled **A comparative study of personal values profile of rural and urban adolescents.** The present research study was conducted to assess the personal values profile of rural and urban adolescents randomly selected (18-20 yrs.) from four Colleges of Punjab Agricultural University, Ludhiana. The socioeconomic status scale was used to study the socio-demographic characteristics of the respondents. Personal values profile of the respondents was assessed by employing personal values questionnaire by Sherry and Verma (2010). The results revealed that significantly higher proportion of urban adolescents were found on the dimensions of 'Religious', 'Democratic' and 'Hedonistic' values whereas rural adolescents were observed significantly higher on the dimensions of 'Family prestige'. Urban adolescents were found to have more faith in God. The results further depicted that urban adolescents believed in individuality and were against any kind of discrimination on the basis of sex, race, caste and family status. They did not believe in social inequality, however, rural adolescents gave more value to family prestige than urban adolescents. Rural adolescents believed in maintenance of purity of family blood by avoiding inter-caste marriages. Urban boys gave more value to power and desired to rule or lead others and preferred a job where they could get opportunity to exercise authority over others.

2.5 SUMMARY:

In this present chapter we discussed about importance of literature review. Here we discussed about literature of family environment, happiness, and personal values. We discussed past studies about above topics And importance of literature review. In the next chapter-3, research design is described in brief detail.

CHAPTER 3

RESEARCH METHODOLOGY

3.1 Introduction

3.2 Statement of the Research Problem

3.3 Objectives of the Study

3.4 Hypothesis of the Study

3.5 Methods and procedure

3.5.1 Selection of the Sample

3.5.2 Research Design

3.5.3 Variables of the Study

- **Independent Variables**
- **Dependent Variables**
- **Controlled Variables**

3.5.4 Research Tools

3.5.4.1 Personal Information Form

3.5.4.2 Family Environment Scale

3.5.4.3 Happiness Scale

3.5.4.4 Personal Values Scale

3.5.4.5 Technique of Data Collection

3.6 Statistical Analysis

3.7 Summary

3.1 INTRODUCTION:

Research Methodology is systematic way to solve a problem. It is a science of studying how research is to be carried out. Essentially the procedures by which researchers go about their work of describing explaining and predicting phenomena are called research methodology. It is also defined as the study of methods by which knowledge is gained. Its aim is to give the work plan of research.

It is necessary for a researcher to design a methodology for the problem chosen .One should note that even if the method considered in two problems are same the methodology may be different. It is important for the researcher to know not only the research methods necessary for the research under taken but also the methodology.

Research is an essential and powerful tool is leading man towards progress. Without systematic research there would have been very little progress. John W.Best has rightly said "The secret of our cultural development has been research, pushing back the areas of ignorance by discovering new truths, which in turn, lead to better ways of doing things and better products.

Scientific research leads to progress in some field of life. New products, new facts, new concepts and new ways of doing things are being found due to ever increasing significant research in the physical, the biological, the social and the psychological fields. Research today is no longer confined to the science laboratory. The manufacturers, the agricultural experts and the archeologists are carrying on research in their respective spheres, besides, the sociologists, anthropologists, economists and educationists

According to John W. Best,"Research may be defined as the systematic and objective analysis and recording of controlled observation that may lead to the developments of generalizations, principles or theories, resulting in prediction and possibly ultimate control or events".

According to C.C. Crawford "Research is simply a systematic and refined technique of thinking, employing specialized tools, instruments&

procedures in order to obtain a more adequate solution of a problem than would be possible under ordinary means."

According to Rusk "Research is a point of view, an attitude of inquiry or a frame of mind. It asks questions which have hitherto not been asked, and it seeks to answer them by following a fairly definite procedure. It is not a mere theorizing, but rather an attempt to elicit facts and to face them once they have been assembled. Research is likewise not an attempt to bolster up pre-conceived opinions, and it implies a readiness to accept the conclusions to which an inquiry leads, no matter how unwelcome they may prove. When successful, research adds to the scientific knowledge of the subject.

Actually research is simply the process of arriving as dependable solution to a problem through the planned and systematic collection, analysis and interpretation of data. Research is the most important process for advancing knowledge for promoting progress and to enable man to relate more effectively to his environment to accomplish his purpose and to resolve his conflicts. Although it is not the only way, it is one of the more effective ways of solving scientific problems.

3.2 STATEMENT OF THE RESEARCH PROBLEM:

The problem statement is as under:

"Family Environment, Happiness and Personal Values of Individuals Living in Joint Family and Nuclear Family."

3.3 OBJECTIVES OF THE STUDY:

Before joining a research work clearly defined objective directs a researcher in the right direction and the researcher can focus on the study.

The researcher has decided the following objectives.

(1) To study of the difference between the Family Environment score of people in relation to their Type of family. (Joint and Nuclear).

(2) To study of the difference between the Family Environment score of people in relation to their Gender. (Male and Female).

(3) To study of the difference between the Family Environment score of people in relation to their Type of Area.(Urban and Rural)

(4) To study of the Interaction effect between the Family Environment score of people in relation to their Type of Family, Gender, and Type of Area.

(5) To study of the difference between the Happiness score of people in relation to their Type of Family. (Joint and Nuclear).

(6) To study of the difference between the Happiness Score of the people in relation to their Gender (Male and Female).

(7) To study of the difference between the Happiness score of people in relation to their Type of Area (Urban and Rural).

(8) To study of Interaction effect between the Happiness score of people in relation to their Type of Family, Gender, and Type of Area.

(9) To study of the difference between the personal Value score of people in relation to their Type of Family. (Joint and Nuclear).

(10) To study of the difference between the Personal Value score of people in relation to their Gender. (Male and Female).

(11) To study of the difference between the personal Value score of people in relation to their Type of Area. (Urban and Rural).

(12) To study of the difference between the personal Value score of People in relation to their Type of Family, Gender, And Type of Area.

(13) To study of correlation of the Family Environment, Happiness, and Personal value score of people in relation to their Type of Family.(Joint and Nuclear)

(14) To study of correlation of the Family Environment, Happiness and Personal value score of people in relation to their Gender (Male and Female).

(15) To study of correlation of the Family Environment, Happiness and Personal value score of people in relation to their type of Area. (Urban and Rural).

3.4 HYPOTHESIS OF THE STUDY:

Hypothesis is a fundamental and important element of research. If research is done without hypothesis so that it's like running arrow in dark. After the scientific selection of the research problem the researcher constructed the hypothesis.

According to F.M. Kerlinger,

"A hypothesis in a conjectural statement of the relation between two or more variables". Hypothesis can always be expressed in the form of a declarative sentence. And that shows a general and specific relationship between variables.

Hypothesis of the present study were us follows:

1) There will be no significant difference between score of Family Environment of people in relation to their Type of Family. (Joint and Nuclear).
2) There will be no significant difference between score of Family Environment of people in relation to their Gender. (Male and Female).
3) There will be no significant difference between score of Family Environment of people in relation to their Type of Area.(Urban and Rural)
4) There will be no significant difference between score of Family Environment of people in relation to their Type of Family and Gender.
5) There will be no significant difference between score of Family Environment of people in relation to their Type of Family and Type of Area.
6) There will be no significant difference between score of Family Environment of people in relation to their Gender and Type of Area.
7) There will be no significant difference between score of Family Environment of people in relation to their Type of Family, Gender and Type of Area.
8) There will be no significant difference between score of Happiness of people in relation to their Type of Family. (Joint and Nuclear).

9) There will be no significant difference between score of Happiness of people in relation to their type of Gender. (Male and Female).

10) There will be no significant difference between score of Happiness of people in relation to their Type of Area. (Urban and Rural)

11) There will be no significant difference between score of Happiness of people in relation to their Type of Family and Gender.

12) There will be no significant difference between score of Happiness of people in relation to their Type of Family and Type of Area.

13) There will be no significant difference between score of Happiness of people in relation to their Gender and Type of Area.

14) There will be no significant difference between score of Happiness of people in relation to their Type of Family, Gender and Type of Area.

15) There will be no significant difference between score of Personal Value of people in relation to their Type of Family. (Joint and Nuclear).

16) There will be no significant difference between score of Personal Value of people in relation to their Gender. (Male and Female).

17) There will be no significant difference between score of Personal Value of people in relation to their Type of Area. (Urban and Rural)

18) There will be no significant difference between score of Personal Value of people in relation to their Type of Family and Gender.

19) There will be no significant difference between score of Personal Value of people in relation to their Type of Family and Type of Area.

20) There will be no significant difference between score of Personal Value of people in relation to their Gender and Type of Area.

21) There will be no significant difference between score of Personal Value of people in relation to their Type of Family, Gender and Type of Area.

22) There will be no significant correlation between score of Family Environment and Happiness of Joint Family.

23) There will be no significant correlation between score of Family Environment and Personal Value of Joint Family.

24) There will be no significant correlation between score of Happiness and Personal Value of Joint Family.

25) There will be no significant correlation between score of Family Environment and Happiness of Nuclear Family.

26) There will be no significant correlation between score of Family Environment and Personal Value of Nuclear Family.

27) There will be no significant correlation between score of Happiness and Personal Value of Nuclear Family.

28) There will be no significant correlation between score of Family Environment and Happiness of Male.

29) There will be no significant correlation between score of Family Environment and Personal Value of Male.

30) There will be no significant correlation between score of Happiness and Personal Value of Male.

31) There will be no significant correlation between score of Family Environment and Happiness of Female.

32) There will be no significant correlation between score of Family Environment and Personal Value of Female.

33) There will be no significant correlation between score of Happiness and Personal Value of Female.

34) There will be no significant correlation between score of Family Environment and Happiness of Urban Area.

35) There will be no significant correlation between score of Family Environment and Personal Value of Urban Area.

36) There will be no significant correlation between score of Happiness and Personal Value of Urban Area.

37) There will be no significant correlation between score of Family Environment and Happiness of Rural Area.

38) There will be no significant correlation between score of Family Environment and Personal Value of Rural Area.

39) There will be no significant correlation between score of Happiness and Personal Value of Rural Area.

3.5 METHODS AND PROCEDURE:

3.5.1 Selection of the Sample

The random sampling technique was used for selection of sample in this study. The sample of the present study constituted total 320 people out of which 160 were from joint family people (80 male and 80 female) and 160 were from nuclear family people (80 man and 80 female).A total sample of 320 people equally distributed between gender and type of area and type of the family from various areas of Ahmedabad city of Gujarat State selected for this research. For this research 650 samples were collected. Purposive sampling technique will be utilized for the selection of the sample in the study. 2 x 2 x 2 factorial design was used in this research work for study.

Table 3.1

Sample Design

Type Of Area (C)	Type of Family(A)				Total
	Joint Family (A_1)		Nuclear Family (A_2)		
	Gender(B)				
	Male (B_1)	Female (B_2)	Male (B_1)	Female (B_2)	
C_1 Urban	40	40	40	40	160
C_2 Rural	40	40	40	40	160
Total	80	80	80	80	320

Where

A = Type of Family   B= Gender   C = Type of Area

A_1 = Joint Family B_1=Male C_1 = Urban

A_2=Nuclear Family B_2=Female C_2 = Rural

3.5.2 Research Design:

Table No: 3.2

2x2x2 Factorial Design

<table>
<tr><th rowspan="4">Type Of Area (C)</th><th colspan="4">Type of Family(A)</th><th rowspan="4">Total</th></tr>
<tr><th colspan="2">Joint Family (A_1)</th><th colspan="2">Nuclear Family (A_2)</th></tr>
<tr><th colspan="4">Gender(B)</th></tr>
<tr><th>Male (B_1)</th><th>Female (B_2)</th><th>Male (B_1)</th><th>Female (B_2)</th></tr>
<tr><td>C_1 Urban</td><td>$A_1B_1C_1$ n=40</td><td>$A_1B_2C_1$ n=40</td><td>$A_2B_1C_1$ n=40</td><td>$A_2B_2C_1$ n=40</td><td>n=160</td></tr>
<tr><td>C_2 Rural</td><td>$A_1B_1C_2$ n=40</td><td>$A_1B_2C_2$ n=40</td><td>$A_2B_1C_2$ n=40</td><td>$A_2B_2C_2$ n=40</td><td>n=160</td></tr>
<tr><td>Total</td><td>n=80</td><td>n=80</td><td>n=80</td><td>n=80</td><td>N=320</td></tr>
</table>

Where

A = Type of Family B= Gender C = Type of Area

A_1 = Joint Family B_1=Male C_1 = Urban

A_2=Nuclear Family B_2=Female C_2 = Rural

3.5.3 Variables of the Study:

In the present study two types of Family (Joint Family and Nuclear Family), two types of Gender (Male and Female) and two types of Area (Urban and Rural) will be taken as an independent Variables. The row score of Family Environment, Happiness and Personal Values of people will be taken as dependent variables.

❖ **Independent Variables**

Table 3.3

Showing the table of Variables name, type, level and name of levels

Sr. No	**Name of Variables**	**Type of Variables**	**Grade of Level**	**Name of levels**
1	Type of Family	Independent	2	A1 –Joint Family A2-Nuclear Family
2	Gender	Independent	2	B1- Male B2-Female
3	Type of Area	Independent	2	C1-Urban C2-Rural

❖ **Dependent Variables**

Table 3.4

Showing the table of Variables name, type, level and name of levels

Sr No	**Name of Variables**	**Types of Variables**	**Grade of Level**	**Name of levels**
1	Family Environment	Dependent	8	*Relationship Dimensions (1) Cohesion (2) Expressiveness (3) Conflict (4) Acceptance and Caring ***Personal Growth Dimensions** (5)Independence (6)Active-Recreational Orientation ***System maintenance Dimensions** (7)Organization (8)Control
2	Happiness	Dependent	5	(1)Career Well-being (2)Subjective Well-Being (3)Social Well-Being (4)Spiritual Well-Being (5)Emotional Well-Being
3	Personal Values	Dependent	10	(1)Religious Value (2)Social Value

Sr No	Name of Variables	Types of Variables	Grade of Level	Name of levels
				(3)Democratic Value (4)Aesthetic Value (5)economic Value (6)Knowledge Value (7)Hedonistic Value (8)Power Value (9)Family Prestige Value (10)Health Value

- **Controlled variables:**

  (1) In the present study only joint family and nuclear family are included.

  (2) Sample has been taken in a controlled numbers.

  (3) Present study is limited to Ahmedabad city urban and rural area only.

3.5.4 Research Tools:

For conducting this research the following tools were used:

3.5.4.1 Personal information Form:

Keeping in view the objectives in the presented research to receive some personal information personal information form was prepared. in which gender, age ,educational qualification, educational stream, profession, marital status, type of family, type of city, annual income of family such details have been placed.

3.5.4.2 Family Environment scale:

In the present research Family Environment scale (2017) designed by Dr. Harpreet Bhatia & Dr. N. K. Chadha was used. In which 69 sentences were included. This scale was suitable for individual and group testing. The age range of people who respond this test those 17 to 50 years old. People were asked to respond to the items by marking any one of the five response options. Scale is dividing in 8 different dimensions. *Relationship dimensions (1)Cohesion(2)Expressiveness(3)Conflict(4)Acceptance and Caring *Personal

Growth Dimensions (5)Independence (6)Active-Recreational Orientation *System Maintenance Dimensions (7)Organization (8)Control

Reliability:

Present scale was split into two halves. The Scores of each dimension were also split into two halves. The scores for each of these halves were then correlated. From this self-correlation on the half –tests, the reliability coefficient of whole test was estimated using the spearman-Brown prophecy formula. The reliability coefficients thus obtained are as follows:

Sr .No.	Sub-Scales	Reliability Coefficients
I	Cohesion	0.92
II	Expressiveness	0.88
III	Conflict	0.84
IV	Acceptance and Caring	0.86
V	Independence	0.70
VI	Active-Recreational Orientation	0.48
VII	Organization	0.75
VII	Control	0.48

Overall Test Reliability Coefficient=0.95

Validity: Both face and content validity were tested by giving scale to eighteen experts to evaluate the test items, only those items with at least 75 per cent agreement among the judges were retained.

For content validity, the dimensions of the family environment were selected and clearly defined for purpose of measuring the specific aspects of the environment. These definitions were also subjected to the judgement of the eight experts in the first step, and five experts in second step.

Scoring:

The scoring of Family Environment is as under:

Item	Strongly Agree	Agree	Neutral	Disagree	Strongly Disagree
Positive	5	4	3	2	1
Negative	1	2	3	4	5

Norms:

The Qualitative norms for the sample of the age range of 17 to 50 years are presented here:

Sr.No.	Sub-Scales	Raw Score	Qualitative Norms
I	Cohesion	61 and above 46 to 60 45 and below	High Average Low
II	Expressiveness	40 and above 28 to 39 27 and below	High Average Low
III	Conflict*	52 and above 38 to 51 37 and below	Low conflict Average Conflict High conflict
IV	Acceptance and Caring	55 and above 41 to 54 40 and below	High Average Low
V	Independence	41 and above 31 to 40 30 and below	High Average Low
VI	Active-Recreational Orientation	34 and above 26 to 33 25 and below	High Average Low
VII	Organization	10 7 to 9 6 and below	High Average Low
VIII	Control	18 and above 14 to 17 13 and below	High Average Low

*In this sub-scale, high score is indicative of low conflict and vice versa.

3.5.4.3 Happiness Scale:

Happiness scale (2017) constructed by Dr. Himanshi Rastogi and Dr. Janki Moorjani. The scale consist 62 items divided in 5 different Factors. (1)Career Well-being (2) Subjective Well-being (3) Social Well-being (4) Spiritual Well-Being (5) Emotional Well-being. The responses of the scale are Strongly Agree, Agree, and Undecided, Disagree, Strongly Disagree. Happiness scale has 62 statements and all statements has positive manner. For try out this scale (by developers) the first Draft of 92 items in the scale was given to a randomly selected sample of 120 youths in the age range of 18 to 40 years, male and female. The minimum to maximum range of scoring table was 62 to 310

Reliability:

The Reliability of scale was calculated on basis of split-half (odd-even method).it was Calculated to be r = 0.88 which is significant at .01 level of significance.

Validity :

The items were validated with an external criteria test Subjective Happiness Scale, Which is likert scale as well , the correlation was calculated to be r = 0.91.

Scoring:

The scoring system was as following table.

Nature of Item	Strongly Agree	Agree	Undecided	Disagree	Strongly Disagree
Positive	5	4	3	2	1

Norms for interpretation of the Level of Happiness

Sr. no.	Area-wise Raw Score Range					Full Scale Raw Score Range	Grade	Level of Happiness
	Career	Subjective	Social	Spiritual	Emotional			
1	63 & more	63 & more	53 & more	53 & more	59 & more	288 & more	A	Extremely High
2	57-62	56-62	46-40	46-52	51-57	254-287	B	High
3	50-56	50-55	40-45	39-45	43-50	220-253	C	Above Average
4	41-49	40-49	31-39	29-38	34-22	174-219	D	Average
5	35-40	34-39	25-30	22-28	26-33	140-173	E	Below Average
6	29-34	27-33	18-24	15-21	19-25	106-139	F	Low
7	28 & less	26 &less	17 & less	14 & less	18 & less	105&less	G	Extremely Low

Higher the score, the better is the level of well-being and Happiness.

3.5.4.4 Personal Values Scale:

Personal Values Scale(2017) constructed by Dr. (Mrs.) G .P. Sherry and Prof. R. P. Verma. the scale consist 40 items divided in 10 Factors(1)Religious value(2)Social value(3)Democratic value(4)Aesthetic value (5)Economic value (6)Knowledge value(7)Hedonistic value(8)Power value(9)Family prestige value(10)Health value.

❖ **INSTRUCTION FOR FILLING OUT THE PVQ**

The instructions for filling out the questionnaire are given on page 1 of PVQ. The investigator should read them carefully and assure himself that he has followed them.

❖ **ADMINISTRATION OF PVQ**

PVQ may be administered individually as well as in a group. It should be filled out under the standard instructions. First the respondent should fill up the personal data blank printed on the front page. But they should be clearly instructed not to fill up the cage which is meant for the investigator. When all the respondents have filled up the blank they should be asked to turn over the page. The investigator should read out the instructions printed on page 1 of the PVQ – loudly and clearly. The respondents should follow him carefully. He should explain the mode of filling out the PVQ very carefully, preferably with the help of a black board if one is available there. When he is sure that they have understood the mode of recording their responses, he should permit them to turn over the page, and ask them to record their responses .He should invigilate the respondents while they are filling up the PVQ lest they should consult one another.

1. The formula has been given by Wert et al. (1954)

2. The advantage of fixing these limits for the popularity value was that in weighting the response categories as 2 (most preferred), 1 (intermediately preferred), 3 (least preferred) on the basis of sealing there was very small error of approximation.

3. The N was 310

- **SCORING OF THE PVQ**

The responses are to be scored as follows:

(1)2 for tick mark showing the most preferred value under the stem.

(2)0 for a cross showing the least preferred value under the stem.

(3)1 for the blank or unmarked item showing the intermediate preference for the value.

Values	Most Preferred value	Least Preferred Value	Not Preferred Value
Score	2	0	1

Sometimes the respondents leave some questions unanswered. If the number of such questions is 4 or less, each item of the unanswered question should be scored as 1. If their number is more than 4 the questionnaire should be rejected.

In all the cases the scores should be recorded beside the corresponding bracket and the total for each value (A to Z) should be written in the cage given at the foot of the page. The correctness of scoring and recording of the totals for all the values is checked by summing the total for all of them on each page separately. If the grand total is 24 the scoring may be correct, provided that compensating errors have not been committed.

Finally the entries in the cage at the foot of each page should be should be brought to the bigger cage on the cover page of the PVQ. The total of each column should be noted down in the bottom row. These totals denote the scores of the respondent on the corresponding value given at the top of the column. In this questionnaire.

1	A	Religious Value
2	B	Social Value
3	C	Democratic Value
4	D	Aesthetic Value
5	E	Economic Value
6	F	Knowledge Value
7	G	Hedonistic Value
8	H	Power Value
9	I	Family Prestige Value
10	J	Health Value

INTERPRETATION OF THE DEVIDED SCORES

In order to interpret the derived scores, it is essential to fix up the score-bounds for the qualitative categories. There is no universally accepted mode of conversion of the quantitative data into qualitative ones. Here an arbitrary scheme of conversions is given, but it may be considered as satisfactory for most purposes.

INTERPRETATION OF DERIVED SCORES

T-Scores	Sten Scores	Grade	Interpretation
65 and above	9 and 10	A	Very High Value
55-64	7 and 8	B	High Value
46-54	5 and 6	C	Average Value
35-45	3 and 4	D	Low Value
34 and below	2 and 1	E	Very Low Value

VALIDITY VIA CORRELATION

Although validity coefficients are liable to be deceptive and should not be accepted yet they prove to be useful indices of validity if the heterogeneity of sample and other factors are kept in view in obtaining them. The validity of PVQ was obtained by finding out the hierarchy of values of sample of 20 psychology students of B. A. Parl II in two ways. Firstly they were administered PVQ and the hierarchy of their ten values was determined. Then they were asked to rank the ten values. The ten values were functionally defined in terms of the contents of the PVQ. The two hierarchies were correlated and the rank order coefficient of correlation of .64 was found. This correlation is significant at .05 level (df = 8).Thus it is may be said that the PVQ is a fairly valid tool to determine the hierarchy of values of a group. It may be remarked here that the foregoing evidence of the validity of PVQ are fairly strong.

RELIABILITY

Reliability of a tool is generally defined as the ratio of true variance to the scores (Guilford). The error variance component of the scores generated by perfectly reliable tool is zero and there is no error of measurement. Hence reliability is one of the most important characteristics of a tool which denotes how accurately the tool measures whatever it measures.

Two indices of reliability of PVQ were found out. Firstly, its reliability was determined by Hoyt's method using analysis of variance which method is as efficient as Kuder Richardson's but less cumbersome. Secondly, two test-retest reliabilities were determined one after an interval of 11 month and other of 3 months. Thus three sets of reliability coefficients for the PVQ are available at present and they are presented in table below.

Indices of Reliability of PVQ

Sr. No.	VALUES	Test –retest Reliabilities		Analysis variance reliabilities (N=50)	Standard error of measurements
		Time gap 11 Months (N=48)	Time gap 3 months (N=50)		
1	Religious Value	.52	.82	.64	1.6
2	Social value	.45	.66	.47	1.9
3	Democratic value	.62	.57	.48	2.4
4	Aesthetic Value	.47	.65	.56	1.8
5	Economic Value	.67	.70	.70	2.0
6	Knowledge Value	.59	.63	.50	2.2
7	Hedonistic Value	.61	.54	.63	2.0
8	Power Value	.55	.53	.60	2.1
9	Family Prestige Value	.57	.85	.67	1.6
10	Health value	.53	.64	.52	2.2

3.5.4.5 Technique of Data Collection:

The process of Data collection is the soul of the any research plan. To get reliable and accurate information first of all met with the head of the family obtained prior approval and aware of the purpose of study the study. After that the head of family in the allotted time limit interviewed face to face with family members. After that by clarifying the importance of the study and its purpose tried to win their trust. Then fill in the personal information form by giving proper instruction and gave a proper understanding of how to give answers in the tests received their responses from family members.

3.6 STATISTICAL ANALYSIS:

Considering the variables of the present study analysis of variance (ANOVA), and correlation was used for main and interactive effect of three variables. ANOVA (2x2x2 factorial design) used for this study. Hypotheses were tested at 0.05 and 0.01 levels of significance. F test was selected to interpret the results obtained in the investigation to find out the significant difference in variables of the study. Statistical analysis for 2x2x2 factorial design was done with the help of computer and manually.

3.7 SUMMARY:

Thus in this chapter considering the research method we studied about the Objectives, Variables, sample, Hypothesis, Tools, procedure and statistical analysis of this research study.

Now in the next chapter will come under the results and interpretation of the research study.

CHAPTER- 4
ANALYSIS AND INTERPRETATIONS OF THE DATA

4.1 INTRODUCTION

The present chapter is considered to be the heart of the entire research report. In order to draw conclusions from the information collected during the entire research work, it is very important to interpret the information accurately and correctly.

According to Croxton and Cowden,

"Statistics may be defined as the collection, presentation, analysis, and interpretation of numerical data."

According to Bowleg,

"Statistics may rightly be called the science of averages."

According to Prof. Horace secrist,

"Aggregates of facts affected to a marked extent by multiplicity of causes, numerically expressed, enumerated or estimated according to reasonable standards of accuracy, collected in a systematic manner for a predetermined purpose and placed in relation to each other".

- ❖ The distribution of information in this chapter is done with the hypothesis in mind in such a way that thc analysis of the information becomes meaningful.
- ❖ The formulas required for statistical calculations are used.
- ❖ After performing statistical analysis the interpretation is presented in the form of findings.
- ❖ The researcher also used indexes and graphs to present the information in a high and accurate manner.

4.2 RESULTS AND DISCUSSIONS

4.2.1 'F' Value Results and Discussions

Table 4(A):-

Showing 'F' Value of different groups in relation to Family Environment of people

Source of Variance	Df	SS	Mss=ss/df	'F' value	Significance level
SS_A	1	738.1125	738.1125	2.76	N.S.
SS_B	1	5797.0125	5797.0125	21.75	0.01
SS_C	1	5248.8	5248.8	19.69	0.01
SS_{AxB}	1	26901.1125	26901.1125	100.94	0.01
SS_{AxC}	1	22.05	22.05	0.08	N.S.
SS_{BxC}	1	105.8	105.8	0.39	N.S.
SS_{AxBxC}	1	732.05	732.05	2.74	N.S.
SS_{Error}	312	83145.25	266.49	-	-
SS_{Total}	319	-	-	-	-

* 0.05 level table value=3.87

** 0.01 level table value=6.72

Table- 4.1

Showing Mean, 'F' value of Family Environment of people in relation to type of family

	Type of family (A)		'F' value	Level of Significance
	Joint (A1)	Nuclear (A2)		
Mean	241.675	238.6375	2.76	N.S.
N	160	160		

The table shows mean score and 'F' value of family environment of joint and nuclear family. The mean score of joint family is 241.675 and the mean value of nuclear family is 238.6375. The F value is 2.76. So there is no significant difference between score of family environment of people in relation to their type of family. The Hypothesis no.1 "There will be no significant difference between score of family environment of people in relation to their type of family (Joint and Nuclear)" is accepted.

It is concluded that the score of family environment among the joint family and nuclear family both are same.

Graph 4.1

Showing Bar Graph with Mean scores, 'F' value of Family Environment of people in relation to their Type of Family.

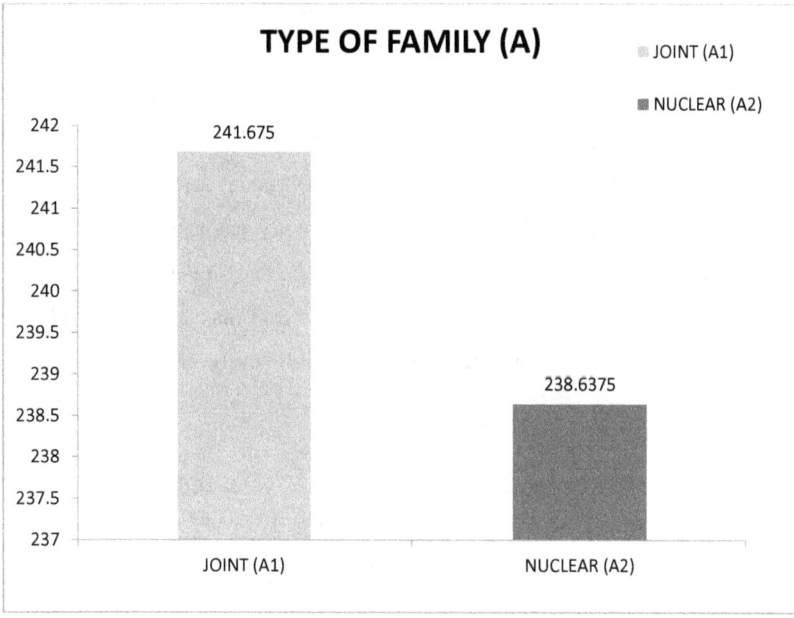

Graph No. 4.1 show that the family environment of the people at type of family joint family and nuclear family score are same.

Table- 4.2

Showing Mean, 'F' value of Family Environment of people in relation to the Type of Gender

	Gender (B)		'F' value	Level of Significance
	Male (B1)	Female (B2)		
Mean	244.4125	235.9	21.75	0.01
N	160	160		

The table shows mean score and 'F' value of family environment of male and female. The mean score of male is 244.4125 and the mean score of female is 235.9. The 'F' value is 21.75 which is significant at 0.01 level. So there is significant difference between score of family environment of people in relation to their Type of Gender and Hypothesis No 2 "There will be no significant difference between score of Family environment of people in relation to their Type of Gender (Male and Female) is rejected.

It is concluded that the score of Family environment among Male and Female the score of male persons higher than female Persons.

The reason of higher score of man persons may due to our Indian culture. In Indian culture male persons have good family environment than female persons.

Graph 4.2

Showing Bar Graph with Mean scores, 'F' value of Family Environment of people in relation to their Type of Gender.

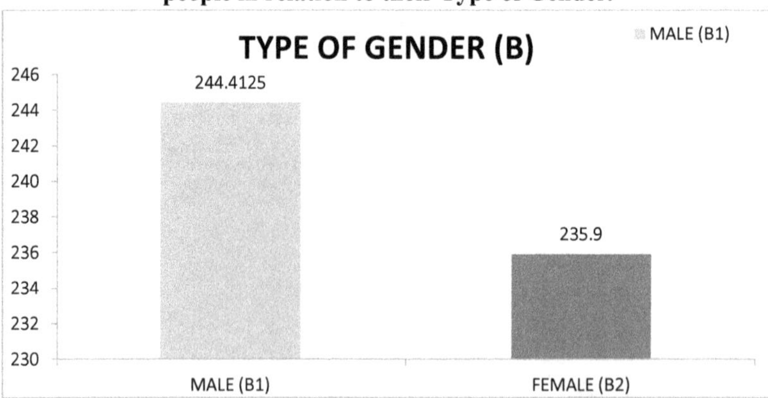

Graph no.4.2 show that the family environment of the people at type of gender male person has higher family environment than female person.

Table- 4.3

Showing Mean, 'F' value of Family Environment of people in relation to the Type of Area

	Area (C)		'F' value	Level of Significance
	Urban (C1)	Rural (C2)		
Mean	236.10625	244.20625	19.69	0.01
N	160	160		

The table shows mean score and 'F' value of family environment of urban area and rural area. The mean score of urban area is 236.10625 and the mean score of rural area is 244.20625. The 'F' value is 19.69 which is significant at level 0.01. so there is significant difference between score of family environment of people in relation to their Type of Area and Hypothesis No 3 "There will be no significant difference between score of family environment of people in relation to their area (Urban and Rural) is rejected.

It is concluded that the score of family environment among Urban and Rural area the score of Rural Area higher than Urban Area.

The reason of this result is in the villages, people live in harmony with each other and everyone is respected. Supporting each other in every situation. So the family environment in the village is better than in the city.

Graph 4.3

Showing Bar Graph with Mean scores, 'F' value of Family Environment of people in relation to their Type of Area.

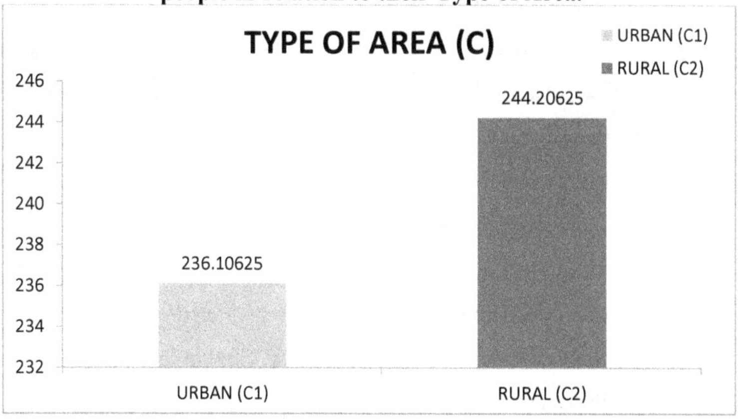

Graph No-4.3 show that the family environment of people at Type of area rural area has a high score than urban area.

Table- 4.4

Showing Mean, 'F' value of Family Environment of people in relation to the Type of Family and Type of Gender

	Type of Family (A)				**'F' value**	**Level of Significance**
	Joint (A1)		**Nuclear (A2)**			
	Gender(B)		**Gender(B)**			
	Male (B1)	**Female (B2)**	**Male (B1)**	**Female (B2)**		
Mean	255.1	228.25	233.725	243.55	100.94	0.01
N	80	80	80	80		

The table shows mean score and 'F' value of family environment of both type of family and gender. The mean score of A_1B_1 is 255.1, the mean score of A_1B_2 is 228.25, the mean score of A_2B_1 is 233.725 and mean score of A_2B_2 is 243.55. The 'F' value is 100.94 which is significant at level 0.01. so there is significant difference between score of family environment of people in relation to their Type of Family and Gender and the Hypothesis No 4" There will be no significant difference between score of family environment of people in relation to their Type of Family (Joint and Nuclear) and Type of Gender(Male and Female)" is rejected.

It is concluded that the score of family environment among jointfamily male higher than nuclear family male. Joint family female score lower than nuclear family female.

The reason of this result is men in a joint family are not overly concerned and they are relaxed in every way. When women have to work all day. Women do not have time for themselves. In a nuclear family, the responsibility of the house falls on the men and leisure time is not found. While women are allowed to act in their own way. So that in a joint family men get a good family environment while in a nuclear family women get a good family environment.

Graph 4.4

Showing Bar Graph with Mean scores, 'F' value of Family Environment of people in relation to their Type of Family and Type of Gender.

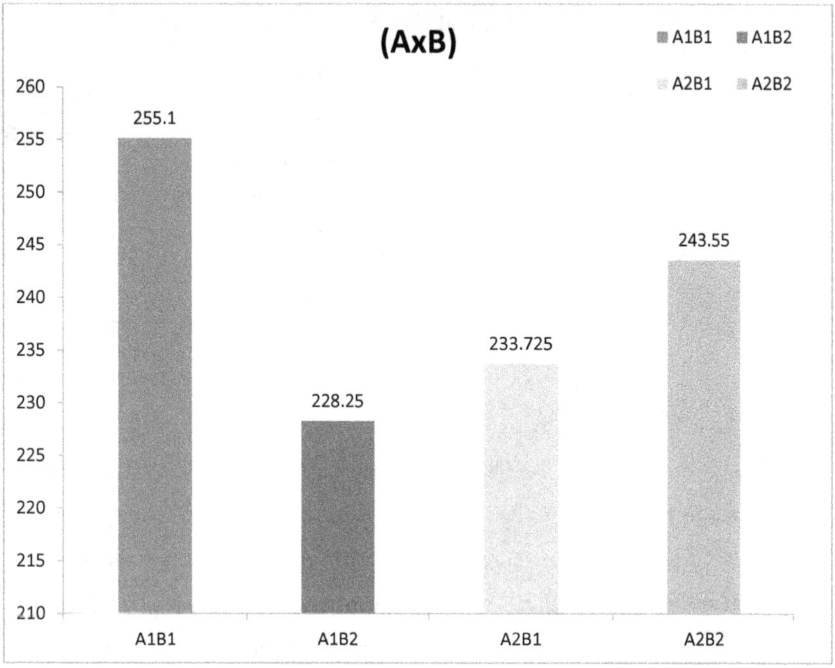

Graph No 4.4 show that the family environment of people, joint family male has higher score than female. And joint family female score has lower than nuclear family.

Table- 4.5

Showing Mean, 'F' value of Family Environment of people in relation to the Type of Family and Area

	Type of Family (A)				**'F' value**	**Level of Significance**
	Joint (A1)		**Nuclear (A2)**			
	Area(C)		**Area(C)**			
	Urban (C1)	**Rural (C2)**	**Urban (C1)**	**Rural (C2)**		
Mean	237.3625	245.9875	234.85	242.425	0.08	N.S.
N	80	80	80	80		

The table shows mean score and 'F' value of family environment of both Type of Family and Area. The mean score of A_1C_1 is 237.3625, the mean score of A_1C_2 is 245.9875, the mean score of A_2C_1 is 234.85 and the mean score of A_2C_2 is 242.425. The 'F' value is 0.08. so there is no significant difference between score of family environment of people in relation to their Type of Family and Type of Are and the Hypothesis No 5 "There will be no significant difference between score of family environment of people in relation to their Type of Family (Joint and Nuclear) and Type of Area (Urban and Rural)" is accepted.

It is concluded that the family environment score among people at Type of family (Joint and Nuclear) and Type of Area (Urban and Rural) both are same.

The reason of this result is day by day the distinction between villages and cities is slowly being erased. The villagers have turned to the culture of the city. There are a lot of changes in families now. So now it is difficult for us to tell the difference.

Graph 4.5

Showing Bar Graph with Mean scores, 'F' value of Family Environment of people in relation to their Type of Family and Type of Area.

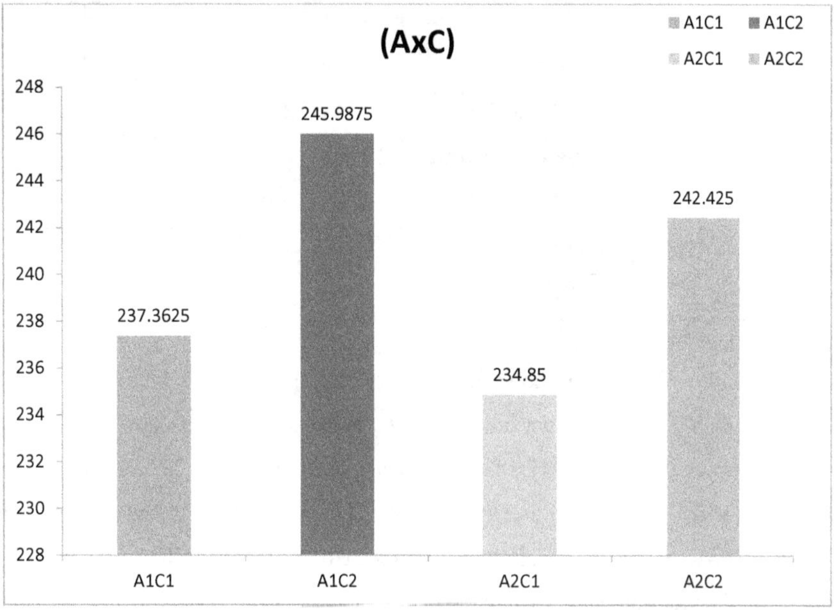

Graph No 4.5 show that the family environment of people, joint family and nuclear family The joint family and the nuclear family living in the city and in the village all have the same score.

Table- 4.6

Showing Mean, 'F' value of Family Environment of people in relation to the Type of Gender and Type of Area

<table>
<tr><th rowspan="4"></th><th colspan="4">Gender (B)</th><th rowspan="4">'F' value</th><th rowspan="4">Level of Significance</th></tr>
<tr><th colspan="2">Male (B1)</th><th colspan="2">Female (B2)</th></tr>
<tr><th colspan="2">Area (C)</th><th colspan="2">Area (C)</th></tr>
<tr><th>Urban (C1)</th><th>Rural (C2)</th><th>Urban (C1)</th><th>Rural (C2)</th></tr>
<tr><td>Mean</td><td>240.9375</td><td>247.8875</td><td>231.275</td><td>240.525</td><td rowspan="2">0.39</td><td rowspan="2">N.S.</td></tr>
<tr><td>N</td><td>80</td><td>80</td><td>80</td><td>80</td></tr>
</table>

The table shows mean score and 'F' value of family environment of both Type of Gender and Area. The mean score of B_1C_1 is 240.9375, the mean score of B_1C_2 is 247.8875, the mean score of B_2C_1 is 231.275, the mean score of B_2C_2 is 240.525 and the 'F' value is 0.39.so there is no significant difference between score of family environment of people in relation to their Type of Gender and Type of Area. The Hypothesis No 6 "There will be no significant difference between score of family environment of people in relation to their Type of Gender (Male and Female) and Type of Area (Urban and Rural)" is accepted.

It is concluded that the family environment score among people at Type of Gender (Male and Female) and Type of Area (Urban and Rural) both are same.

The reason of this is in this time men and women are moving to distant cities for their business. Even in the villages, the effect of urban culture is slowly being seen and its direct effect is also seen on the family atmosphere there.

Graph 4.6

Showing Bar Graph with Mean scores, 'F' value of Family Environment of people in relation to their Type of Gender and Type of Area.

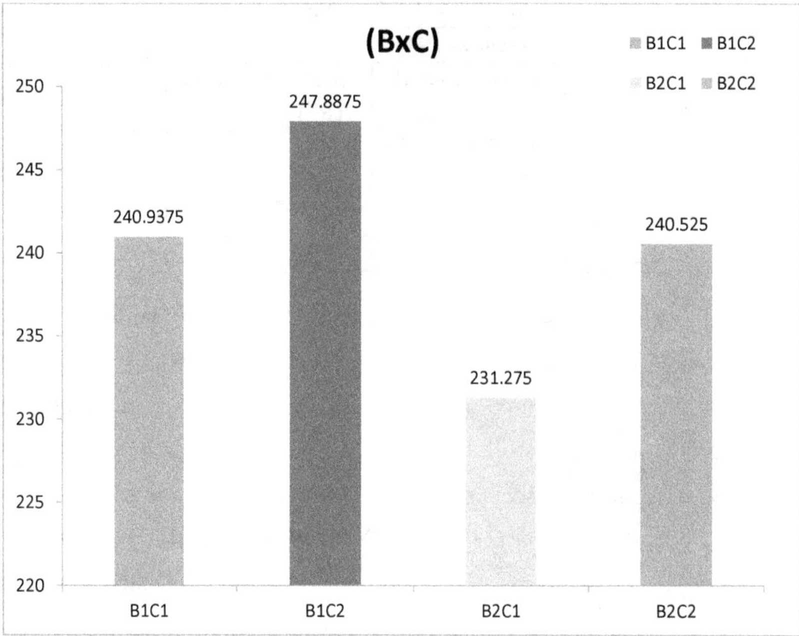

Graph No 4.6 show that the family environment of people, the scores of men and women living in rural and urban areas are similar.

Table- 4.7

Showing Mean, 'F' value of Family Environment of people in relation to the Type of Family, Gender and Area

Area (C)		Type of Family (A)				'F' value	Level of Significance
		Joint (A1)		Nuclear (A2)			
		Gender (B)		Gender (B)			
		Male (B1)	Female (B2)	Male (B1)	Female (B2)		
Urban (C1)	Mean	249.85	224.875	232.025	237.675	2.74	N.S.
	N	40	40	40	40		
Rural (C2)	Mean	260.35	231.625	235.425	249.425		
	N	40	40	40	40		

The table shows mean score and 'F' value of family environment of Type of Family, Gender and Area of people. The mean score of $A_1B_1C_1$ is 249.85, the mean score of $A_1B_1C_2$ is 260.35, the mean score of $A_1B_2C_1$ is 224.875, the mean score of $A_1B_2C_2$ is 231.625, the mean score of $A_2B_1C_1$ is 232.025, the mean score of $A_2B_1C_2$ is 235.425, the mean score of A_2B_2C1 is 237.675, The mean score of $A_2B_2C_2$ is 249.425 and the 'F' value is 2.74 so there is no significant difference between score of family environment of people in relation to their Type of Family, Gender and Area. The Hypothesis No 7 "There will be no significant difference between score of family environment of people in relation to their Type of Family, Gender and Area" is accepted.

It is concluded that the family environment score among people at Type of Family (Joint and Nuclear), Type of Gender (Male and Female) and Type of Area (Urban and Rural) are same.

The reason of this result is today the distinction between village and city is being erased. Men and women have been given equal status. There have also been changes in the form of joint families and nuclear families. The number of nuclear families exceeds the number of joint families. Because of Corona, people have come to understand the importance of family.

Graph 4.7

Showing Bar Graph with Mean scores, 'F' value of Family Environment of people in relation to their Type of Family, Gender and Area

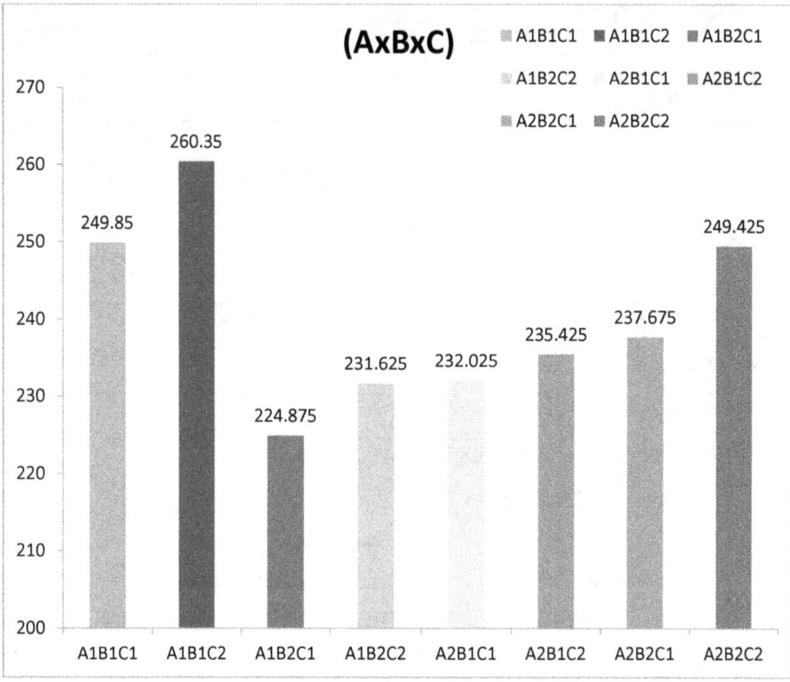

Graph No 4.7 show that family environment of people, men and women living in villages and cities who live in a joint or nuclear families have the same scores.

Table 4(B):-

Showing 'F' Value of different groups in relation to Happiness of people

Source of Variance	Df	SS	Mss=ss/df	'F' value	Significance level
SS_A	1	714.0125	714.0125	2.78	N.S.
SS_B	1	3948.05	3948.05	15.42	0.01
SS_C	1	13494.0125	13494.0125	52.72	0.01
SS_{AxB}	1	85936.05	85936.05	335.75	0.01
SS_{AxC}	1	2279.1125	2279.1125	8.90	0.01
SS_{BxC}	1	2856.05	2856.05	11.15	0.01
SS_{AxBxC}	1	3036.8	3036.8	11.86	0.01
SS_{Error}	312	79858.4	255.95	-	-
SS_{Total}	319	-	-	-	-

* 0.05 level table value=3.87

** 0.01 level table value=6.72

Table- 4.8

Showing Mean, 'F' value of Happiness of people in relation to Type of Family

	Type of Family (A)		'F' value	Level of Significance
	Joint (A1)	Nuclear (A2)		
Mean	234.925	231.9375	2.78	N.S.
N	160	160		

The table shows mean score and 'F' value of happiness of Joint and Nuclear Family. The mean score of joint family is 234.925. The mean score of nuclear family is 231.9375. The 'f' value is 2.78. So there is no significant difference between score of happiness of people in relation to their type of family. The Hypothesis No 8 "There will be no significant difference between score of happiness of people in relation to their Type of Family (Joint and Nuclear) "is accepted.

It is concluded that the score of happiness among people at Type of Family (Joint and Nuclear) are same.

Graph 4.8

Showing Bar Graph with Mean scores, 'F' value of Happiness of people in relation to their Type of Family.

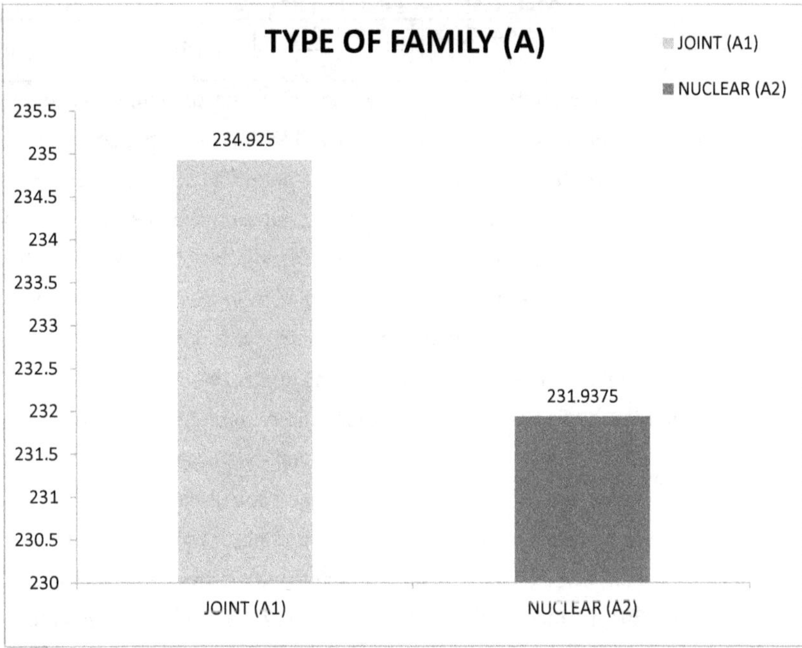

Graph No 4.8 show that the happiness of people at type of family joint family and nuclear family scores are same.

Table- 4.9
Showing Mean, 'F' value of Happiness of people in relation to the Type of Gender

	Gender (B)		'F' value	Level of Significance
	Male (B1)	Female (B2)		
Mean	236.94375	229.91875	15.42	0.01
N	160	160		

The table shows mean score and 'F' value of happiness of male and female. The mean score of male is 236.94375 and the mean score of female is 229.91875. The 'F' value is 15.42 which is significant at 0.01 level. So there is significant difference between score of happiness of people in relation to their Gender and The Hypothesis No 9 "There will be no significant difference between score of happiness of people in relation to their Type of Gender (Male and Female)" is rejected. It is concluded that the score of happiness among male and Female the score of male persons higher than female persons.

The reason of this result is in Indian culture, men have a responsibility only to earn. They are allowed to hang out as well as all other types. While women have to take care of all the household responsibilities. Many women are involved in business as well as child care and household chores. Thus men are happier than women. This result is match with previous research by Komal Vyas (2020) A Study fo the Happiness Among the Students with References to thier education level and gender.

Graph 4.9
Showing Bar Graph with Mean scores, 'F' value of Happiness of people in relation to their Type of Gender.

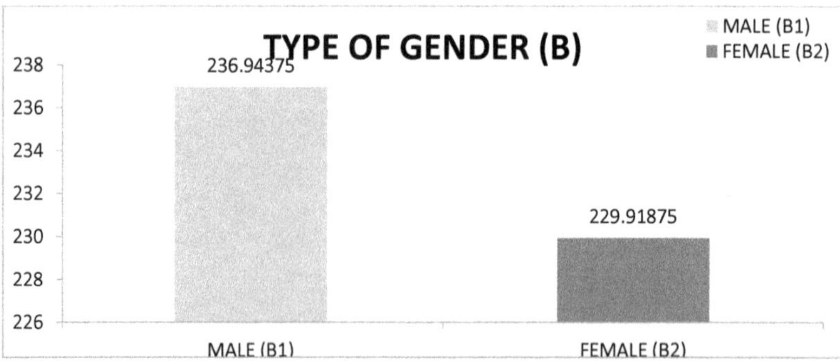

Graph No 4.9 shows that the happiness of the people at type of gender male persons has higher score than female persons. Male persons happier than female persons.

Table- 4.10

Showing Mean, 'F' value of Happiness of people in relation to the Type of Area

	Area (C)		'F' value	Level of Significance
	Urban (C1)	Rural (C2)		
Mean	226.9375	239.925	52.72	0.01
N	160	160		

The table shows mean score and 'F' value of happiness of urban and rural area. The mean score of urban area is 226.9375 and the mean score of rural area is 239.925. The 'F' value is 52.72 which is significant at level 0.01.so there is significant difference between score of happiness of people in relation to their Type of Area and Hypothesis No 10 "There will be no significant difference between score of happiness of people in relation to their Type of Area(Urban and Rural)" is rejected.

It is concluded that the score of happiness among Urban and Rural area the score of rural area higher than urban area.

The reason of this result is the people of the city are falling prey to many diseases in the pursuit of material happiness. Which is why they can't be happy. While the villagers live a relatively contented and peaceful life. So that they are relatively happier than the citizens.

Graph 4.10

Showing Bar Graph with Mean scores, 'F' value of Happiness of people in relation to their Type of Area

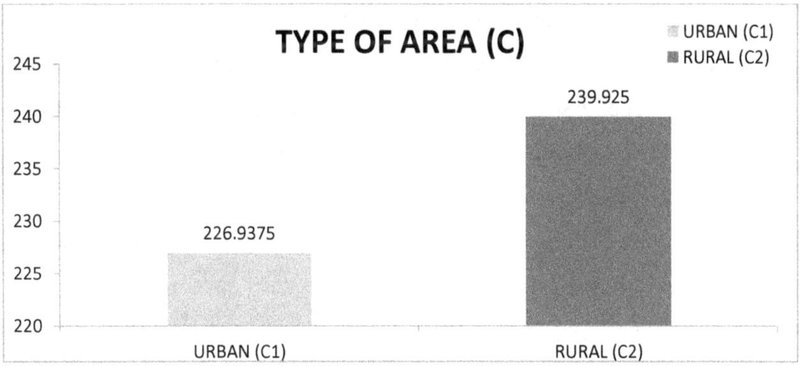

Graph No- 4.10 shows that the happiness of people at type of area, urban area score lower than rural area.

Table- 4.11

Showing Mean, 'F' value of Happiness of people in relation to the Type of Family and Gender

<table>
<tr><th rowspan="4"></th><th colspan="4">Type of Family (A)</th><th rowspan="4">'F' value</th><th rowspan="4">Level of Significance</th></tr>
<tr><th colspan="2">Joint (A1)</th><th colspan="2">Nuclear (A2)</th></tr>
<tr><th colspan="2">Gender(B)</th><th colspan="2">Gender(B)</th></tr>
<tr><th>Male (B1)</th><th>Female (B2)</th><th>Male (B1)</th><th>Female (B2)</th></tr>
<tr><td>Mean</td><td>254.825</td><td>215.025</td><td>219.0625</td><td>244.8125</td><td rowspan="2">335.75</td><td rowspan="2">0.01</td></tr>
<tr><td>N</td><td>80</td><td>80</td><td>80</td><td>80</td></tr>
</table>

The table shows mean score and 'F' value of happiness of both Type of Family and Gender. The mean score of A_1B_1 is 254.825, the mean score of A_1B_2 is 215.025, the mean score of A_2B1 is 219.0625, and the mean score of A_2B_2 is 244.8125. The 'F' value is 335.75 which is significant at level 0.01.so there is significant difference between score of happiness of people in relation to their Type of Family and Type of Gender and Hypothesis No 11 "There will be no significant difference between score of happiness of people relation to their Type of Family (Joint and Nuclear) and Type of Gender (Male and Female)" is rejected.

It is concluded that score of happiness among type of family and type of gender the score of joint family male higher than nuclear family male. And score of joint family female lower than nuclear family female.

The reason of this result is men are happier in joint families. Because they do not have full responsibility on their own. So they get to spend time with the kids and other family members after they get home from work.

In a nuclear family, the man alone is responsible for meeting the household expenses. So they have to work harder and don't have time for any other work. So that they appear less happy in a nuclear family.

In a joint family, women are burdened with work all day long. They do not get a chance to do the work of their choice. So that women in a joint family appear less happy.

While in a nuclear family women have the opportunity to act according to their choice. So that women from nuclear families tend to be happier in proportion.

Graph 4.11

Showing Bar Graph with Mean scores, 'F' value of Happiness of people in relation to their Type of Family and Gender.

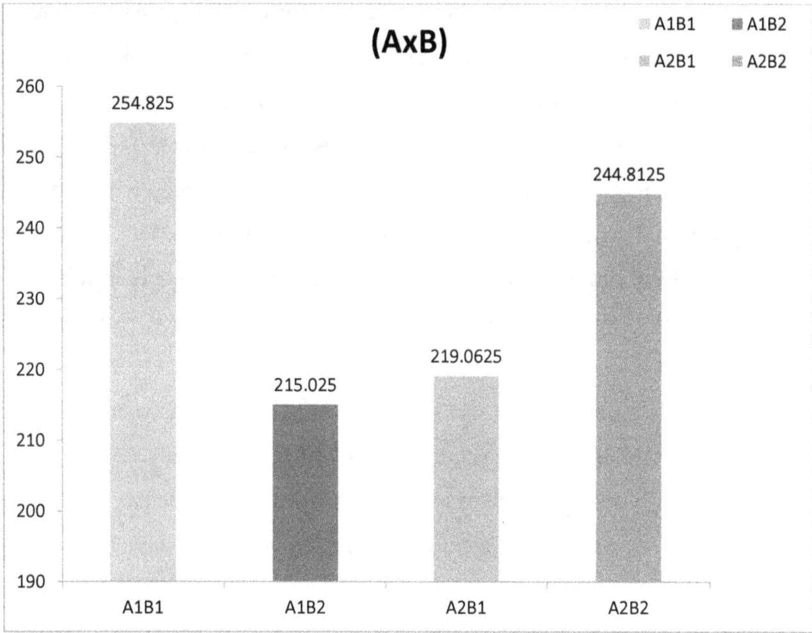

Graph No- 4.11 shows that the happiness of people, joint family male persons has higher score than female persons. Nuclear family female persons has higher score than male persons.

Table- 4.12

Showing Mean, 'F' value of Happiness of people in relation to the Type of Family and Area

	Type of Family (A)				**'F' value**	**Level of Significance**
	Joint (A1)		**Nuclear (A2)**			
	Area(C)		**Area(C)**			
	Urban (C1)	**Rural (C2)**	**Urban (C1)**	**Rural (C2)**		
Mean	225.7625	244.0875	228.1125	235.7625	8.90	0.01
N	80	80	80	80		

The table shows mean score and 'F' value of happiness of both Type of Family and Area. The mean score of A_1C_1 is 225.7625, the mean score of A_1C_2 is 244.0875, the mean score of A_2C_1 is228.1125, the mean score of A_2C_2 is 235.7625. The 'F' value is 8.90 which is significant at 0.01 level. So there is significant difference between score of happiness of people in relation to their Type of Family and type of Area and Hypothesis No 12 "There will be no significant difference between score of happiness of people in relation to their Type of Family (Joint and Nuclear) and Type of Area (Urban and Rural)"is rejected.

It is concluded that rural areas family have a high score of both type of family. And urban areas score lower of both type of family.

The reason of this result of joint families and nuclear families living in villages are happier than families living in cities. Because rural life is more peaceful than urban life.

Graph 4.12

Showing Bar Graph with Mean scores, 'F' value of Happiness of people in relation to their Type of Family and Type of Area.

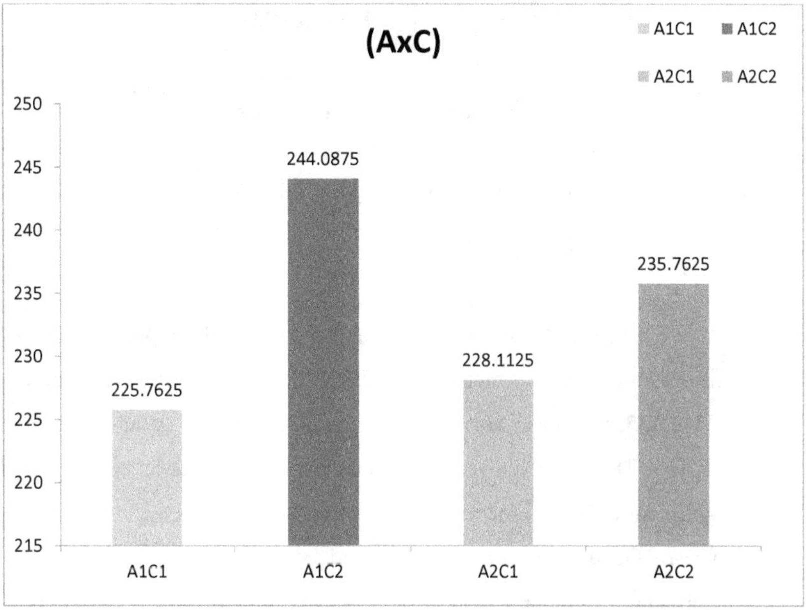

Graph No- 4.12 show that the happiness of people, rural areas family has a high score of both type of family. And urban areas score lower of both type of family.

Table- 4.13

Showing Mean, 'F' value of Happiness of people in relation to the Gender and Type of Area

	Gender (B)				**'F' value**	**Level of Significance**
	Male (B1)		**Female (B2)**			
	Area (C)		**Area (C)**			
	Urban (C1)	**Rural (C2)**	**Urban (C1)**	**Rural (C2)**		
Mean	227.4625	246.425	226.4125	233.425	11.15	0.01
N	80	80	80	80		

The table shows mean score and 'F' value of happiness of both type of Gender and Area. The mean score of B_1C_1 is 227.4625, the mean score of B_1C_2 is 246.425, the mean score of B_2C_1 is 226.4125, the mean score of B_2C_2 is 233.425. The 'F' value is 11.15 which is significant at level 0.01. So there is significant difference between score of happiness of people in relation to their Type of Gender and Type of Area and Hypothesis No 13 "There will be no significant difference between score of happiness of people in relation to their Type of Gender (Male and Female) and Type of Area (Urban and Rural)" is rejected.

It is concluded that score of rural area is higher in both type of Gender. And score of urban area is lower in both type of gender.

The reason of this result is women and men living in villages are relatively happier than women and men living in cities. In rural areas men and women have less workload. While both men and women living in the city have a heavier workload.

Graph 4.13

Showing Bar Graph with Mean scores, 'F' value of Happiness of people in relation to their Type of Gender and Type of Area.

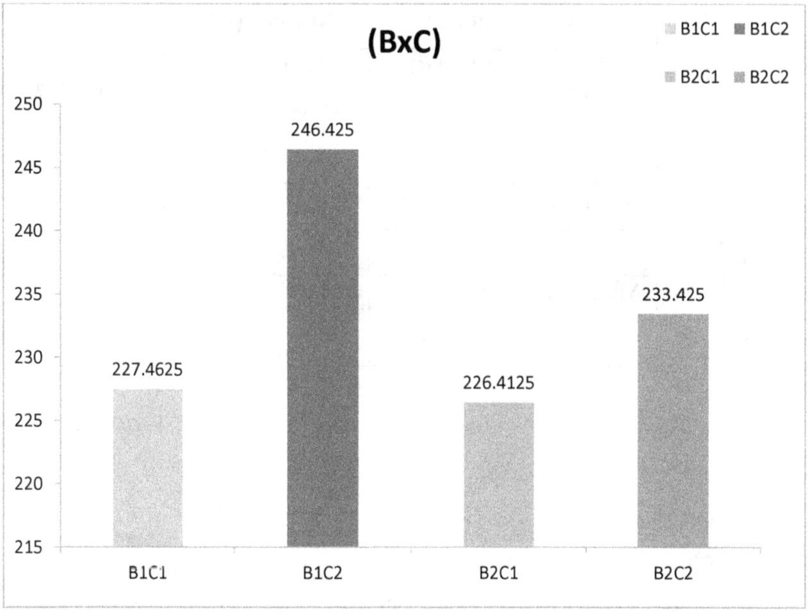

Graph No 4.13 shows that the happiness of people, score of rural area is higher in both type of Gender and score of urban area is lower in both type of gender.

Table- 4.14

Showing Mean, 'F' value of Happiness of people in relation to the Type of Family, Gender and Area

Area (C)		Type of Family (A)				'F' value	Level of Significance
		Joint (A1)		Nuclear (A2)			
		Gender (B)		Gender (B)			
		Male (B1)	Female (B2)	Male (B1)	Female (B2)		
Urban (C1)	Mean	240.875	210.65	214.05	242.175	11.86	0.01
	N	40	40	40	40		
Rural (C2)	Mean	268.775	219.4	224.075	247.45		
	N	40	40	40	40		

The table shows mean score and 'F' value of happiness of Type of Family, Gender and Area. The mean score of $A_1B_1C_1$ is 240.875, the mean score of $A_1B_1C_2$ is 268.775, the mean score of $A_1B_2C_1$ is 210.65, the mean score of $A_1B_2C_2$ is 219.4, the mean score of $A_2B_1C_1$ is 214.05, the mean score of $A_2B_1C_2$ is 224.075, the mean score of $A_2B_2C_1$ is 242.175, the mean score of $A_2B_2C_2$ is 247.45. the 'F' value is 11.86 which is significant at level 0.01. so there is significant difference between score of happiness of people in relation to their Type of Family, Gender and Area. Hypothesis No 14"There will be no significant difference between score of happiness of people in relation to their Type of Family (Joint and Nuclear), Gender (Male and Female) and Area (Urban and Rural)" is rejected.

It is concluded that score of happiness among people at Type of Family (Joint and Nuclear), Type of Gender (Male and Female) and Type of Area (Urban and Rural) are different.

The reason of this result is People living in villages are relatively happier than people living in cities. People living in a nuclear family are relatively happier than those living in a joint family. Women tend to be happier in a nuclear family. While men are found happier in a joint family.

Graph 4.14

Showing Bar Graph with Mean scores, 'F' value of Happiness of people in relation to their Type of Family, Gender and Type of Area.

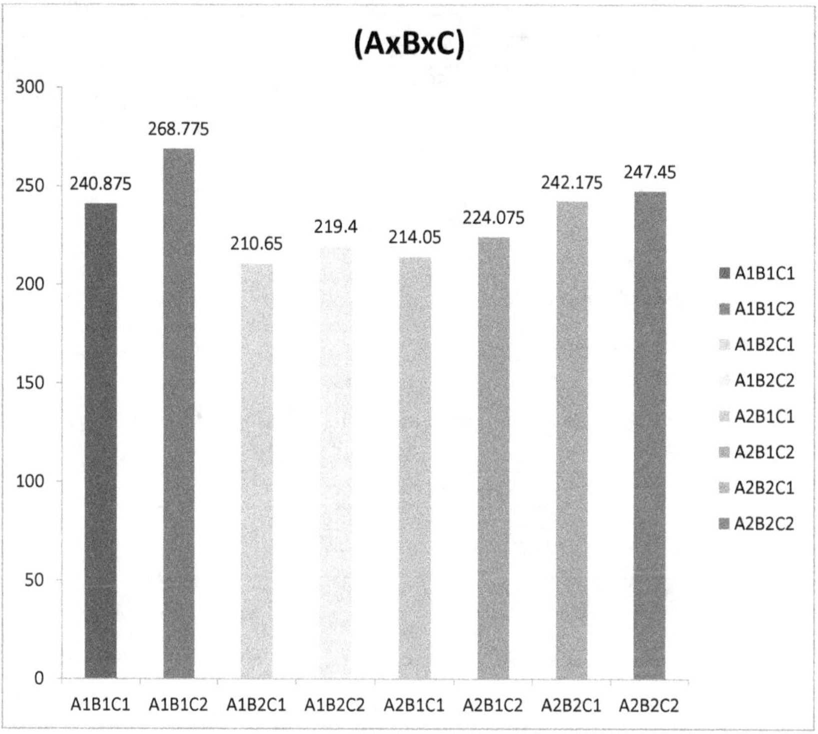

Graph No- 4.14 shows that happiness of people at joint family, nuclear family, male persons, female persons, urban area, rural area score are different.

Table 4(C):-
Showing 'F' Value of different groups in relation to Personal Values of people

Source of Variance	Df	SS	Mss=ss/df	'F' value	Significance level
SS_A	1	613.27813	613.27813	4.40	0.05
SS_B	1	8090.25313	8090.25313	58.05	0.01
SS_C	1	20.50313	20.50313	0.14	N.S.
SS_{AxB}	1	6670.37812	6670.37812	47.86	0.01
SS_{AxC}	1	346.52812	346.52812	2.48	N.S.
SS_{BxC}	1	3491.40312	3491.40312	25.05	0.01
SS_{AxBxC}	1	33.1531	33.1531	0.23	N.S.
SS_{Error}	312	43482.12503	139.365	-	-
SS_{Total}	319	-	-	-	-

* 0.05 level table value=3.87

** 0.01 level table value=6.72

Table- 4.15
Showing Mean, 'F' value of Personal Values of people in relation to Type of Family

	Type of family (A)		'F' value	Level of Significance
	Joint (A1)	Nuclear (A2)		
Mean	100.31875	97.55	4.40	0.05
N	160	160		

The table shows mean score and 'F' value of personal values of Joint family and Nuclear family. The mean score of joint family is 100.31875, the mean score of nuclear family is 97.55. The 'F' value is 4.40 which is significant at 0.05 level. So there is significant difference between score of personal values of people in relation to their Type of Family. Hypothesis No15" There will be no significant difference between score of personal values of people in relation to their Type of Family (Joint and Nuclear)" is rejected.

It is concluded that score of personal values among Type of Family, Joint family score is higher than nuclear family.

The reason of this result is individual values are not maintained in a joint family. Not everyone's opinion is taken there. The decision is made by the head of the household. Whereas in a nuclear family the personal value of the individual is maintained.

Graph 4.15

Showing Bar Graph with Mean scores, 'F' value of Personal Values of people in relation to their type of family.

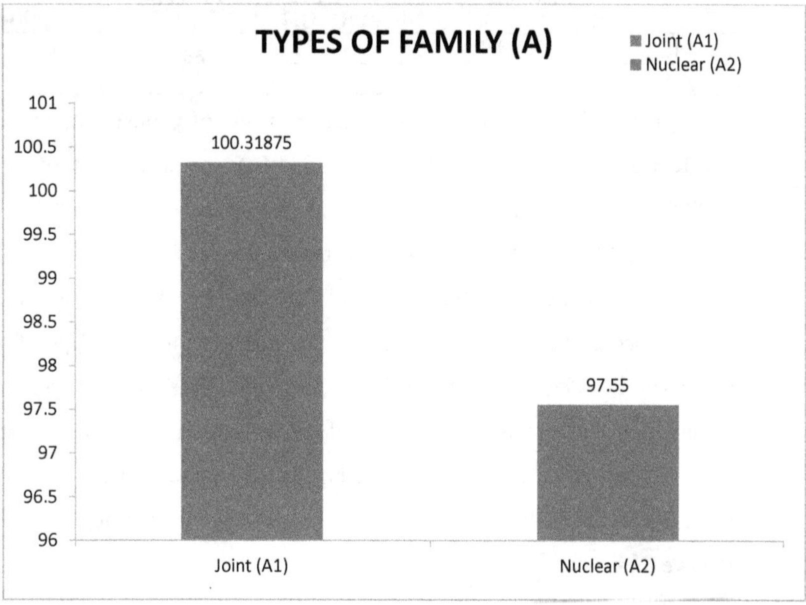

Graph No-4.15 shows that the personal value of people, Joint family score is higher than nuclear family.

Table- 4.16

Showing Mean, 'F' value of Personal Values of people in relation to the Type of Gender

	Gender (B)		'F' value	Level of Significance
	Male (B1)	Female (B2)		
Mean	103.9625	93.90625	58.05	0.01
N	160	160		

The table shows mean score and 'F' value of personal values of male and female. The mean score of male is 103.9625, the mean score of female is 93.90625. The 'F' value is 58.05 which is significant at 0.01 level. So there is significant difference between score of personal values of people in relation to their type of gender. Hypothesis No 16 "There will be no significant difference between score of personal values of people in relation to their Type of Gender (Male and Female)" is rejected. It is concluded that the score of personal values among male and female the score of male persons higher than female persons.

The reason of this result is with male dominance in the Indian family system, only decisions made by men at home are valid. Women have no right to have their say.

Graph 4.16

Showing Bar Graph with Mean scores, 'F' value of Personal Values of people in relation to their type of Gender.

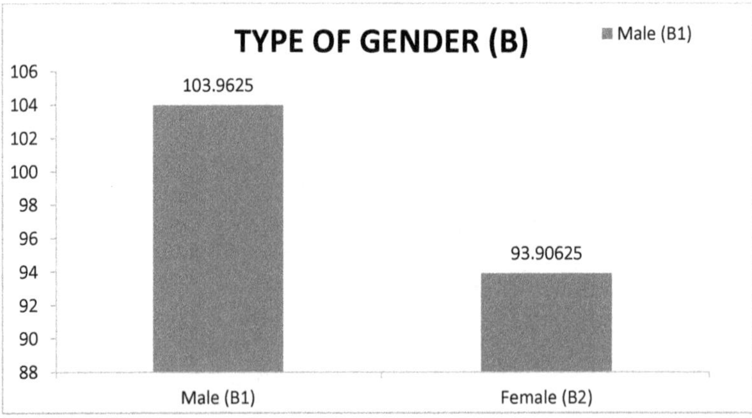

Graph No- 4.16 shows that the personal values of people, among male and female the score of male persons higher than female persons.

Table-4.17

Showing Mean, 'F' value of Personal Values of people in relation to the Type of Area

	Area (C)		'F' value	Level of Significance
	Urban (C1)	Rural (C2)		
Mean	99.1875	98.68125	0.14	N.S.
N	160	160		

The table shows mean score and 'F' value of personal values of Urban and Rural area. The mean score of urban area is 99.1875, the mean score of rural area is 98.68125. The 'F' value is 0.14. so there is no significant difference between score of personal values of people in relation to their Type of Area. The Hypothesis No 17 "There will be no significant difference between score of personal values of people in relation to their Type of Area (Urban and Rural)" is accepted. It is concluded that the personal values score among type of Area are same.

The reason of this result is now days the people of the village have started adopting a culture. So it is difficult to distinguish between rural and urban people.

Graph 4.17
Showing Bar Graph with Mean scores, 'F' value of Personal Values of people in relation to their Type of Area

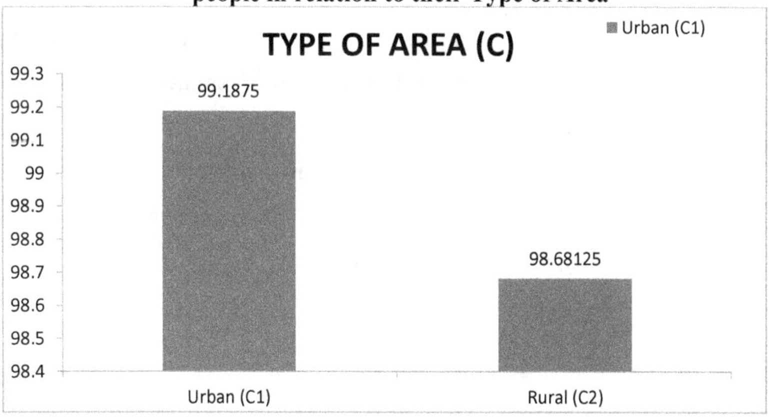

Graph No- 4.17 shows that the personal values of people, urban area score and rural area score are same.

Table-4.18

Showing Mean, 'F' value of Personal Values of people in relation to the Type of Family and Gender

	Type of Family (A)				**'F' value**	**Level of Significance**
	Joint (A1)		**Nuclear (A2)**			
	Gender(B)		**Gender(B)**			
	Male (B1)	**Female (B2)**	**Male (B1)**	**Female (B2)**		
Mean	109.9125	90.725	98.0125	97.0875	47.86	0.01
N	80	80	80	80		

The table shows mean score of personal values of both type of family and gender. The mean score of A_1B_1 is 109.9125, the mean score of A_1B_2 is 90.725, the mean score of A_2B_1 is 98.0125, the mean score of A_2B_2 is 97.0875 and the 'F' value is 47.86 which is significant at level 0.01. so there is significant difference between score of personal values of people in relation to their type of family and type of gender and Hypothesis No 18 "There will be no significant difference between score of personal values of people in relation to their Type of Family (Joint and Nuclear) and Type of Gender (Male and Female)" is rejected

It is concluded that the personal values score among Type of family and type of gender are different. In both types of families, the score of males is higher than that of females.

The reason of this result is in a joint family only the personal values of men are taken into consideration. While in a nuclear family, women have the opportunity to express their personal values.

Graph 4.18

Showing Bar Graph with Mean scores, 'F' value of Personal Values of people in relation to their Type of Family and Gender.

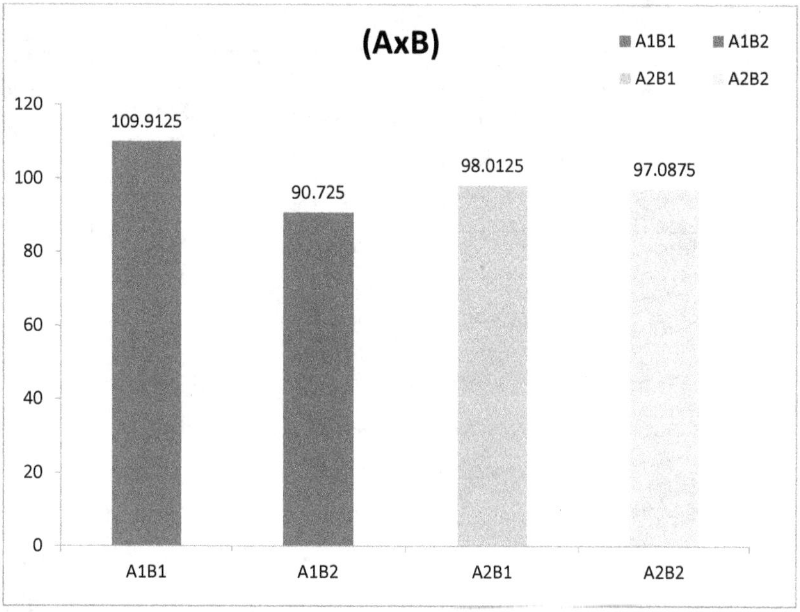

Graph No 4.18 shows that the personal values of people, in both types of families, the score of males is higher than that of females.

Table-4.19

Showing Mean, 'F' value of Personal Values of people in relation to the Type of Family and Area

	Type of Family (A)				**'F' value**	**Level of Significance**
	Joint (A1)		**Nuclear (A2)**			
	Area(C)		**Area(C)**			
	Urban (C1)	**Rural (C2)**	**Urban (C1)**	**Rural (C2)**		
Mean	101.6125	99.025	96.7625	98.3375	2.48	N.S.
N	80	80	80	80		

The table shows mean score and 'F' value of personal values of both type of Family and Area. The mean score of A_1C_1 is 101.6125, the mean score of A_1C_2 is 99.025, the mean score of A_2C_1 is 96.7625, the mean score of A_2C_2 is 98.3375. The 'F' value is 2.48.so there is no significant difference between score of personal values of people in relation to their Type of Family and Type of Area. and Hypothesis No 19 "There will be no significant difference between score of personal values of people in relation to their Type of Family (Joint and Nuclear) and Type of Area (Urban and Rural)" is accepted.

It is concluded that score of personal values of people at Type of Family and Type of area both are same.

The reason of this result is the influence of the culture of the city is being seen across the people from the villages. Which is also showing a change in their personal values then whether it is a joint family or a nuclear family.

Graph 4.19

Showing Bar Graph with Mean scores, 'F' value of Personal Values of people in relation to their Type of Family and Type of Area

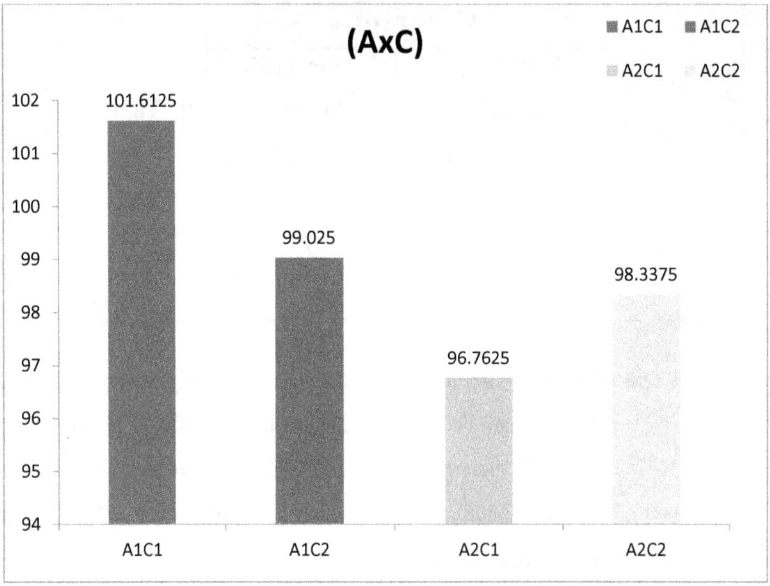

Graph No-19 shows that the personal values of people, joint family and nuclear family, urban area and rural area score are same.

Table- 4.20

Showing Mean, 'F' value of Personal Values of people in relation to their Type of Gender and Type of Area

<table>
<tr><th rowspan="4"></th><th colspan="4">Gender (B)</th><th rowspan="4">'F' value</th><th rowspan="4">Level of Significance</th></tr>
<tr><th colspan="2">Male (B1)</th><th colspan="2">Female (B2)</th></tr>
<tr><th colspan="2">Area (C)</th><th colspan="2">Area (C)</th></tr>
<tr><th>Urban (C1)</th><th>Rural (C2)</th><th>Urban (C1)</th><th>Rural (C2)</th></tr>
<tr><td>Mean</td><td>100.9125</td><td>107.0125</td><td>97.4625</td><td>90.35</td><td rowspan="2">25.05</td><td rowspan="2">0.01</td></tr>
<tr><td>N</td><td>80</td><td>80</td><td>80</td><td>80</td></tr>
</table>

The table shows mean score and 'F' value of personal values of both type of gender and area. The mean score of B_1C_1 is 100.9125, the mean score of B_1C_2 is 107.0125, the mean score of B_2C_1 is 97.4625, the mean score of B_2C_2 is 90.35. The 'F' value is 25.05 which is significant at level 0.01. so there is significant difference between score of personal values of people in relation to their Type of Gender and Type of Area and Hypothesis No 20 "There will be no significant difference between score of personal values of people in relation to their Type of Gender (Male and Female) and Type of Area (Urban and Rural)" is rejected.

It is concluded that score of personal values of people at Type of Gender and Type of Area are different. Men living in villages have higher scores than women.

The reason of this result is Men's personal values are of paramount importance in the village. While women in the city go out to work and are also more educated so that they present their personal values everywhere.

Graph 4.20

Showing Bar Graph with Mean scores, 'F' values of Personal Values of people in relation to their Type of Gender and Type of Area.

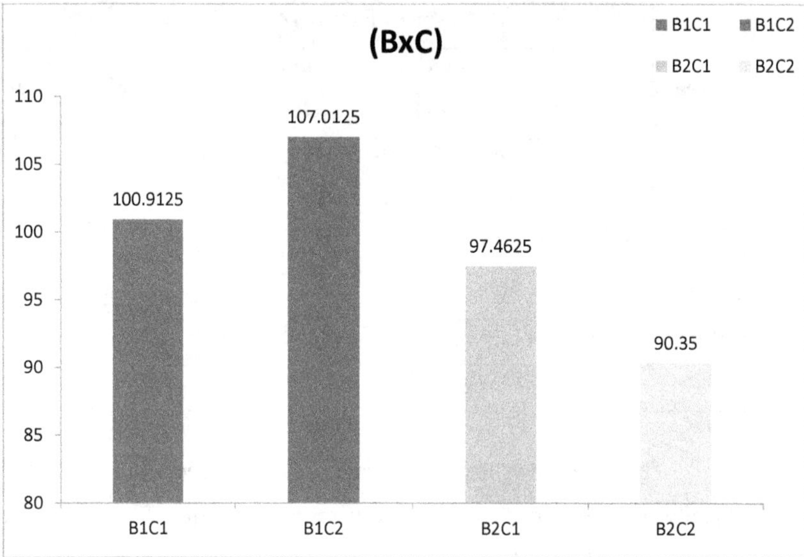

Graph No 20 shows that the personal values of people, men living in villages have higher scores than women.

Table- 4.21

Showing Mean, 'F' value of Personal Values of people in relation to the Type of Family, Gender and Area

<table>
<tr><th rowspan="4">Area
(C)</th><th rowspan="4"></th><th colspan="4">Type of Family (A)</th><th rowspan="4">'F' value</th><th rowspan="4">Level of Significance</th></tr>
<tr><th colspan="2">Joint (A1)</th><th colspan="2">Nuclear (A2)</th></tr>
<tr><th colspan="2">Gender (B)</th><th colspan="2">Gender (B)</th></tr>
<tr><th>Male (B1)</th><th>Female (B2)</th><th>Male (B1)</th><th>Female (B2)</th></tr>
<tr><td rowspan="2">Urban (C1)</td><td>Mean</td><td>108.225</td><td>95</td><td>93.6</td><td>99.925</td><td rowspan="4">0.23</td><td rowspan="4">N.S.</td></tr>
<tr><td>N</td><td>40</td><td>40</td><td>40</td><td>40</td></tr>
<tr><td rowspan="2">Rural (C2)</td><td>Mean</td><td>111.6</td><td>86.45</td><td>102.45</td><td>94.25</td></tr>
<tr><td>N</td><td>40</td><td>40</td><td>40</td><td>40</td></tr>
</table>

The table shows mean score and 'F' value of personal value of Type of Family, Gender and Area. The mean score of $A_1B_1C_1$ is 108.225, the mean score of $A_1B_1C_2$ is 111.6, the mean score of $A_1B_2C_1$ is 95, the mean score of $A_1B_2C_2$ is 86.45, the mean score of $A_2B_1C_1$ is 93.6, the mean score of $A_2B_1C_2$ is 102.45, the mean score of $A_2B_2C_1$ is 99.925, the mean score of $A_2B_2C_2$ is 94.25 and 'F' value is 0.23. so there is no significant difference between score of personal values of people in relation to their type of family, gender and area and Hypothesis No 21 "There will be no significant difference between score of personal values of people in relation to their Type of Family (Joint and Nuclear), Gender (Male and Female) and Area (Urban and Rural)" is accepted.

It is concluded that score of personal values of people at Type of Family, Gender and Area are same.

The reason of this result is Villages are now being transformed into cities. Changes are taking place in the form of joint family and nuclear family. Men and women have been working together in every field.

Graph 4.21

Showing Bar Graph with Mean scores, 'F' value of Personal Values of people in relation to their Type of Family, Gender and Type of Area

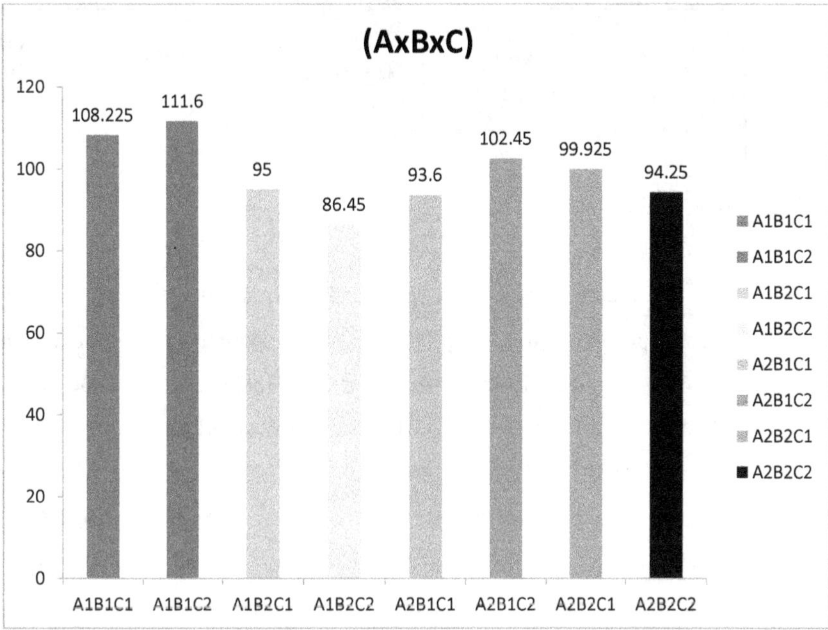

Graph No- 21 shows that the personal values of people, at joint family, nuclear family, male persons, female persons, urban area, rural area score are same.

4.2.2 'r' value Results and Discussion

Table- 4.22
Showing Mean, 'r' value of family environment and happiness of joint family

	Joint Family		'r' value	Level of significance
	Family Environment	Happiness		
Mean	241.675	234.925	0.517726	0.01
N	160	160		

*0.05 Table value=0.161

**0.01 Table value=0.210

The table shows mean score and 'r' value of both family environment and happiness of joint family. The mean score of family environment is 241.675, the mean score of happiness is 234.925. The 'r' value is 0.517726 which is significant at level 0.01. So there is significant correlation is found between family environment and happiness of joint family. The correlation between family environment and happiness was found to be positive. Hypothesis No 22 "There will be no significant correlation between score of family environment and happiness of joint family "is rejected.

Graph 4.22
Showing Bar Graph with Mean scores, 'r' value of Family Environment and Happiness of Joint Family

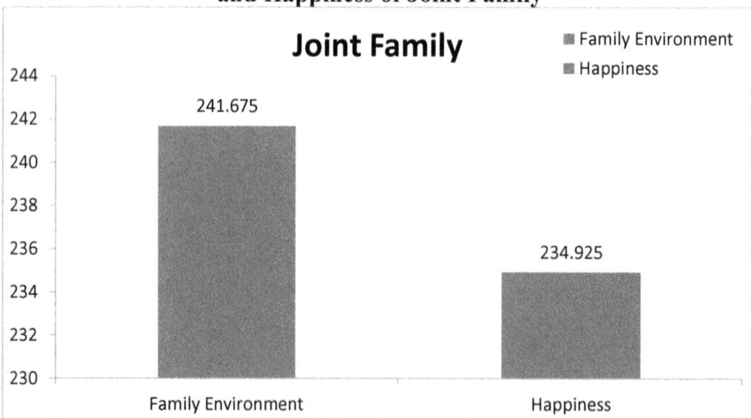

Graph No-22 shows that the family environment and happiness of joint family at family environment is higher than the happiness.

Table- 4.23

Showing Mean, 'r' value of Family Environment and Personal Values of Joint Family

	Joint Family		'r' value	Level of significance
	Family Environment	**Personal values**		
Mean	241.675	100.31875	0.597589	0.01
N	160	160		

*0.05 Table value=0.161

**0.01 Table value=0.210

The table shows mean score and 'r' value of both family environment and personal value of joint family. The mean score of family environment is 241.675, the mean score of personal values is 100.31875. the 'r' value is 0.597589 which is significant at 0.01 level. So there is significant correlation is found between family environment and personal value of joint family. The correlation between family environment and personal value was found to be positive. Hypothesis No 23 "There will be no significant correlation between score of family environment and personal values of joint family" is rejected.

Graph 4.23

Showing Bar Graph with Mean scores, 'r' value of Family Environment and Personal Values of Joint Family.

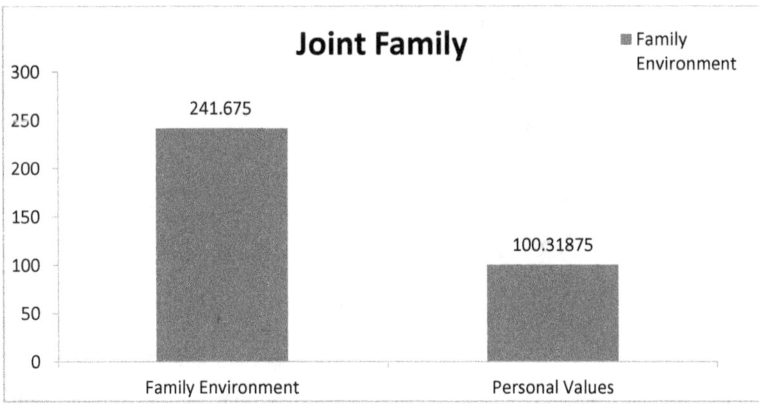

Graph No-23 show that the family environment and personal values of joint family at family environment is higher than the personal values.

Table-4.24

Showing Mean, 'r' value of Happiness and Personal values of Joint Family

	Joint Family		'r' value	Level of significance
	Happiness	Personal values		
Mean	234.925	100.31875	0.464915	0.01
N	160	160		

*0.05 Table value=0.161

**0.01 Table value=0.210

The table shows mean score and 'r' value of both happiness and personal values of joint family. The mean score of happiness is 234.925, the mean score of personal values is 100.31875. the 'r' value is 0.464915 which is significant at 0.01 level. so there is significant correlation is found between happiness and personal values of joint family. The correlation between happiness and personal value was found to be positive. Hypothesis No 24 "There will be no significant correlation between happiness and personal values of joint family" is rejected.

Graph 4.24

Showing Bar Graph with Mean scores, 'r' value of Happiness and Personal Values of Joint Family.

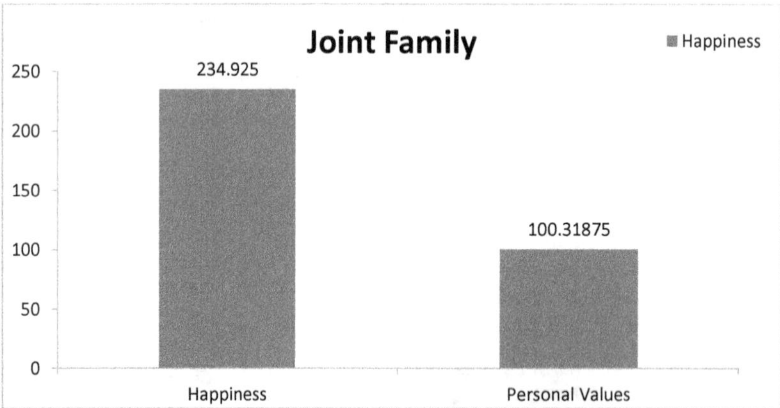

Graph No 24 shows that the happiness and personal values of joint family at happiness is higher than personal values.

Table- 4.25

Showing Mean, 'r' value of Family Environment and Happiness of Nuclear Family

	Nuclear Family		**'r' value**	**Level of significance**
	Family Environment	**Happiness**		
Mean	238.6375	231.9375	0.438569	0.01
N	160	160		

*0.05 Table value=0.161

**0.01 Table value=0.210

The table shows mean score and 'r' value of both family environment and happiness of nuclear family. The mean score of family environment is 238.6375, the mean score of happiness is 231.9375. the 'r' value is 0.438569 which is significant at 0.01 level. so there is significant correlation found between score of family environment and happiness of nuclear family. The correlation between family environment and happiness was found to be positive. Hypothesis No 25 "There will be no correlation between family environment and happiness of nuclear family" is rejected.

Graph 4.25

Showing Bar Graph with Mean scores, 'r' value of Family Environment and Happiness of Nuclear Family.

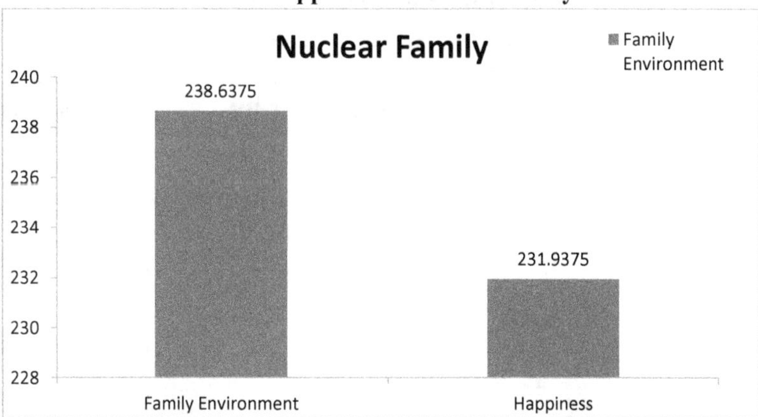

Graph No- 25 shows that the family environment and happiness of nuclear family at family environment and happiness is higher than the happiness.

Table-4.26

Showing Mean, 'r' value of Family Environment and Personal Values of Nuclear Family

	Nuclear Family		'r' value	Level of significance
	Family Environment	Personal Values		
Mean	238.6375	97.55	0.260984	0.01
N	160	160		

*0.05 Table value=0.161

**0.01 Table value=0.210

Table shows mean score and 'r' value of family environment and personal values of nuclear family. The mean score of family environment is 238.6375, the mean score of personal values is 97.55. the 'r' value is 0.260984 which is significant at 0.01 level. so there is significant correlation found between score of family environment and personal values of nuclear family. The correlation was found to be positive. Hypothesis No 26 "There will be no significant correlation between family environment and personal values of nuclear family "is rejected.

Graph 4.26

Showing Bar Graph with Mean scores, 'r' value of Family Environment and Personal Values of Nuclear Family.

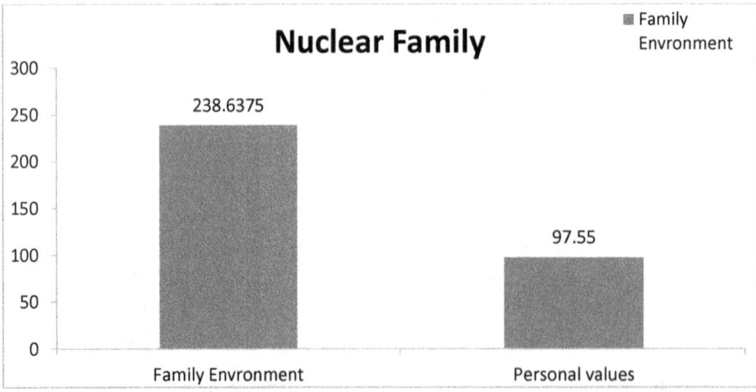

Graph No -26 shows that the family environment and personal values of nuclear family at family environment is higher than the personal values.

Table-4.27

Showing Mean, 'r' value of Happiness and Personal Values of Nuclear Family

	Nuclear Family		'r' value	Level of significance
	Happiness	**Personal Values**		
Mean	231.9375	97.55	0.094545	N.S
N	160	160		

*0.05 Table value=0.161

**0.01 Table value=0.210

The table shows mean score and 'r' value of both happiness and personal values of nuclear family. The mean score of happiness 231.9375, the mean score of personal values is 97.55 and 'r' value is 0.094545. so there is no significant correlation found between score of happiness and personal values. The correlation between happiness and personal values was found to be zero. Hypothesis No 27 "There will be no significant correlation between score of happiness and personal values of nuclear family "is accepted.

Graph 4.27

Showing Bar Graph with Mean scores, 'r' value of Happiness and Personal Values of Nuclear Family.

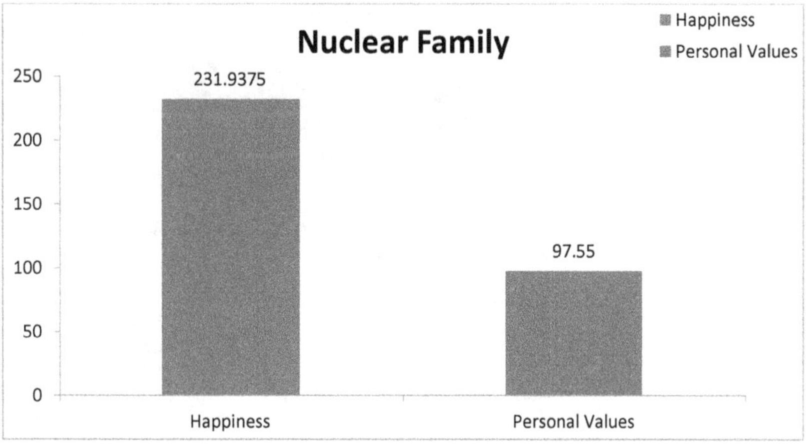

Graph No 27 shows that the happiness and personal values of nuclear family at happiness and personal values have no correlation.

Table-4.28

Showing Mean, 'r' value of Family Environment and Happiness of Male

	Male		'r' value	Level of significance
	Family Environment	Happiness		
Mean	244.4125	236.94375	0.412102	0.01
N	160	160		

*0.05 Table value=0.161

**0.01 Table value=0.210

The table shows mean score and 'r' value of both family environment and happiness of male. The mean score of family environment is 244.4125, the mean score of happiness is 236.94375, the 'r' value is 0.412102 which is significant at 0.01 level. So there is significant correlation found between score of family environment and happiness of male. The correlation between family environment and happiness was found to be positive. Hypothesis No 28 "There will be no significant correlation between family environment and happiness of male" is rejected.

Graph 4.28

Showing Bar Graph with Mean scores, 'r' value of Family Environment and Happiness of Male

Graph No- 28 shows that the family environment and happiness of male at family environment is higher than happiness.

Table- 4.29

Showing Mean, 'r' value of Family Environment and Personal Values of Male

	Male		'r' value	Level of significance
	Family Environment	Personal Values		
Mean	244.4125	103.9625	0.470733	0.01
N	160	160		

*0.05 Table value=0.161

**0.01 Table value=0.210

The table shows mean score and 'r' value of both family environment and personal values of male. The mean score of family environment is 244.4125, the mean score of personal values is 103.9625. the 'r' value is 0.470733 which is significant at 0.01 level. so there is significant correlation found between score of family environment and personal values of male. The correlation between family environment and personal values was found to be positive. Hypothesis No 29 "There will be no significant correlation between score of family environment and personal values of male" is rejected.

Graph 4.29

Showing Bar Graph with Mean scores, 'r' value of Family Environment and Personal Values of Male.

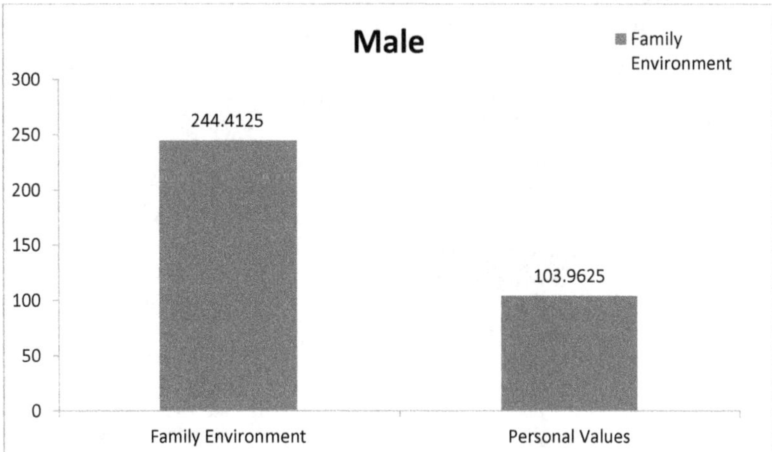

Graph No-29 show that the family environment and personal values of male at family environment is higher than the personal values.

Table-4.30

Showing Mean, 'r' value of Happiness and Personal Values of Male

	Male		'r' value	Level of significance
	Happiness	Personal Value		
Mean	236.94375	103.9625	0.42036	0.01
N	160	160		

*0.05 Table value=0.161

**0.01 Table value=0.210

The table shows mean score and 'r' value of happiness and personal values of male. The mean score of happiness is 236.94375, the mean score of personal value is 103.9625. the 'r' value is 0.42036 which is significant at 0.01 level. so there is significant correlation found between score of happiness and personal values of male. The correlation between happiness and personal values was found to be positive. Hypothesis No 30 "There is no significant correlation between happiness and personal values of male" is rejected.

Graph 4.30

Showing Bar Graph with Mean scores, 'r' value of Happiness and Personal Values of Male.

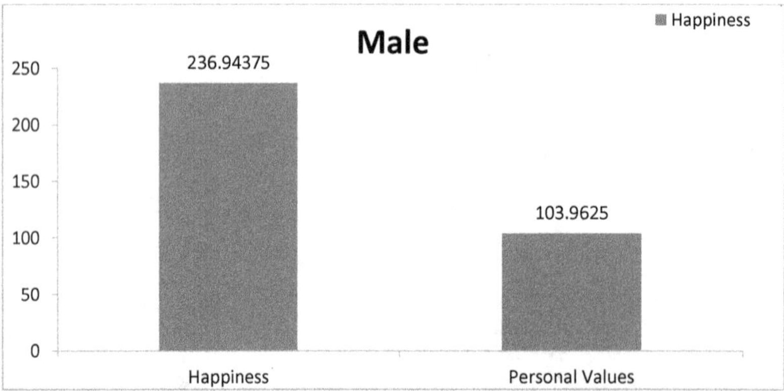

Graph No-30 shows that the happiness and personal values of male at happiness is higher than personal values.

Table- 4.31

Showing Mean, 'r' value of Family Environment and Happiness of Female

	Female		'r' value	Level of significance
	Family Environment	Happiness		
Mean	235.9	229.9	0.538646	0.01
N	160	160		

*0.05 Table value=0.161

**0.01 Table value=0.210

The table shows mean score and 'r' value of both family environment and happiness of female. The mean score of family environment is 235.9, the mean score of happiness is 229.9. the 'r' value is 0.538646 which is significant at 0.01 level. so there is significant correlation found between score of family environment and happiness of female. The correlation between family environment and happiness was found to be positive. Hypothesis No 31 "There will be no significant correlation between score of family environment and happiness of female" is rejected.

Graph 4.31

Showing Bar Graph with Mean scores, 'r' value of Family Environment and Happiness of Female.

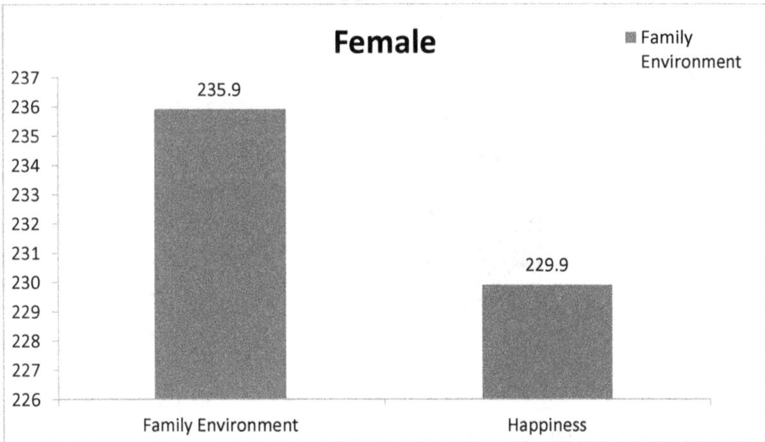

Graph No – 31 shows that the family environment and happiness of female at family environment is higher than happiness.

Table-4.32
Showing Mean, 'r' value of Family Environment and Personal Values of Female

	Female		'r' value	Level of significance
	Family Environment	Personal Values		
Mean	235.9	93.90625	0.4118	0.01
N	160	160		

*0.05 Table value=0.161

**0.01 Table value=0.210

The table shows mean score and 'r' value of both family environment and personal values of female. The mean score of family environment is 235.9, the mean score of personal value is 93.90625. The 'r' value is 0.4118. Which is significant at 0.01 level. So there is significant correlation found between score of family environment and personal values of female. The correlation between family environment and personal values was found to be positive. Hypothesis No 32 "There will be no significant correlation between family environment and happiness of female" is rejected.

Graph 4.32
Showing Bar Graph with Mean scores, 'r' value of Family Environment and Personal Values of Female.

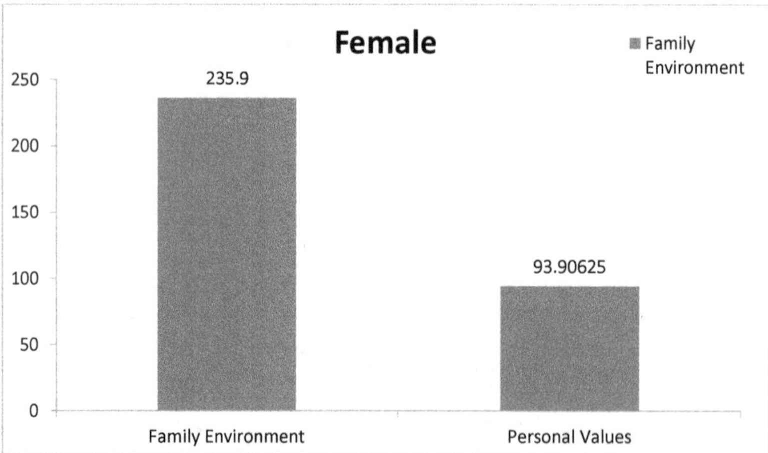

Graph No – 32 show that the family environment and personal values of female at family environment is higher than the personal values.

Table- 4.33

Showing Mean, 'r' value of Happiness and Personal Values of Female

	Female		'r' value	Level of significance
	Happiness	Personal Values		
Mean	229.9	93.90625	0.189108	0.05
N	160	160		

*0.05 Table value=0.161

**0.01 Table value=0.210

The table shows mean score and 'r' value of both happiness and personal values of female. The mean score of happiness is 229.9, the mean score of personal value is 93.90625, the 'r' value is 0.189108 which is significant at 0.05 level. so there is significant correlation between score of happiness and personal values of female. The correlation between happiness and personal values found to be positive. Hypothesis No 33 "There will be no significant correlation between score of happiness and personal values of female "is rejected.

Graph 4.33

Showing Bar Graph with Mean scores, 'r' value of Happiness and Personal Values of Female.

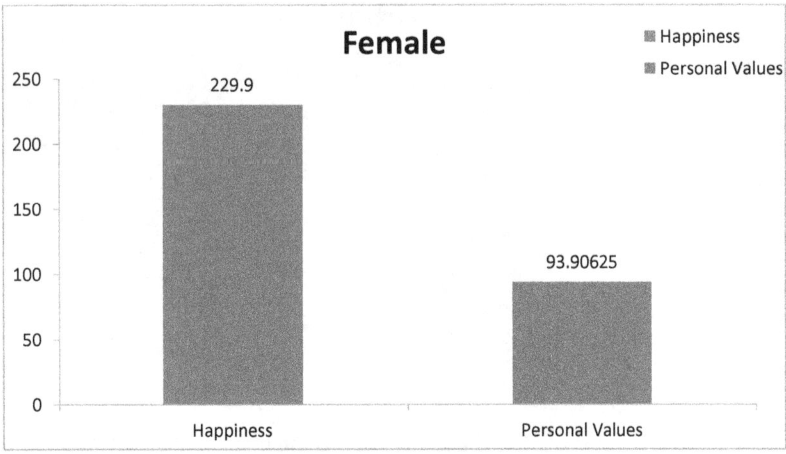

Graph No – 33 shows that the happiness and personal values of fe male at happiness is higher than personal values.

Table- 4.34

Showing Mean, 'r' value of Family Environment and Happiness of Urban Area

	Urban Area		'r' value	Level of significance
	Family Environment	**Happiness**		
Mean	236.10625	226.9375	0.373702	0.01
N	160	160		

*0.05 Table value=0.161

**0.01 Table value=0.210

The table shows mean score and 'r' value of both family environment and happiness of urban area. The mean score of family environment is 236.10625, the mean score happiness is 226.9375. The 'r' value is 0.373702 which is significant at 0.01 level. So there is significant correlation found between score of family environment and happiness of urban area. The correlation between family environment and happiness was found positive. Hypothesis No 34 "There will be no significant correlation between family environment and happiness of urban area "is rejected.

Graph 4.34

Showing Bar Graph with Mean scores, 'r' value of Family Environment and Happiness of Urban Area.

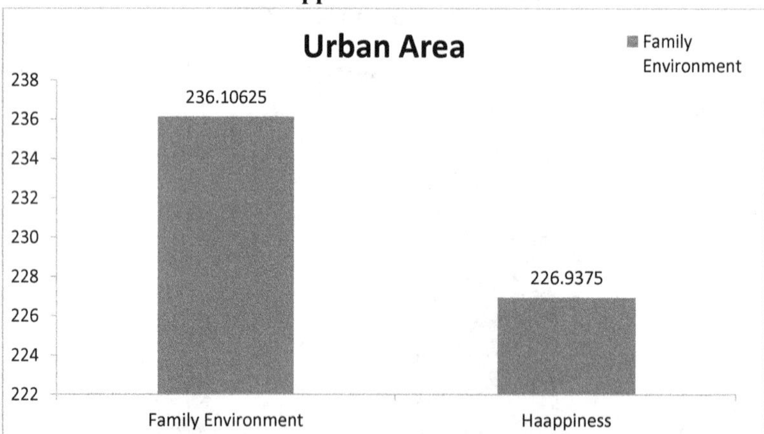

Graph No -34 show that the family environment and happiness of urban area at family environment is higher than the happiness.

Table-4.35
Showing Mean, 'r' value of Family Environment and Personal Values of Urban Area

	Urban Area		'r' value	Level of significance
	Family Environment	Personal Values		
Mean	236.10625	99.1875	0.469786	0.01
N	160	160		

*0.05 Table value=0.161

**0.01 Table value=0.210

The table shows mean score and 'r' value of both family environment and personal values of urban area. The mean score of family environment is 236.10625, the mean score of personal values is 99.1875. the 'r' value is 0.469786. which is significant at 0.01 level. So there is significant correlation found between score of family environment and personal values of urban area. The correlation found between family environment and personal values was found positive. Hypothesis No 35 "There will be no significant correlation between score of family environment and personal values of urban area" is rejected.

Graph 4.35
Showing Bar Graph with Mean scores, 'r' value of Family Environment and Personal Values of Urban Area.

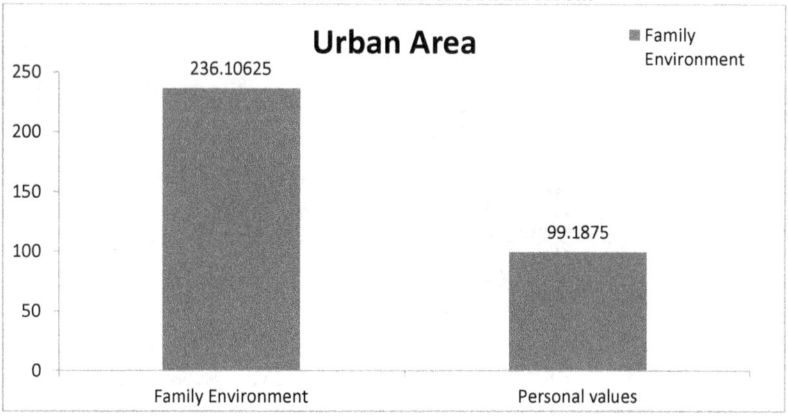

Graph No-35 show that the family environment and personal values of urban area at family environment is higher than the personal values.

Table- 4.36

Showing Mean, 'r' value of Happiness and Personal Values of Urban Area

	Urban Area		'r' value	Level of significance
	Happiness	**Personal Values**		
Mean	226.9375	99.1875	0.332248	0.01
N	160	160		

*0.05 Table value=0.161

**0.01 Table value=0.210

The table shows mean score and 'r' value of both happiness and personal values of urban area. The mean score of happiness is 226.9375, the mean score of personal values is 99.1875, the 'r' value is 0.332248 which is significant at 0.01 level. So there is significant correlation found between score of happiness and personal values of urban area. the correlation between happiness and personal values was found positive. Hypothesis No 36 "There will be no significant correlation between score of happiness and personal values of urban area " is rejected

Graph 4.36

Showing Bar Graph with Mean scores, 'r' value of Happiness and Personal Values of Urban Area.

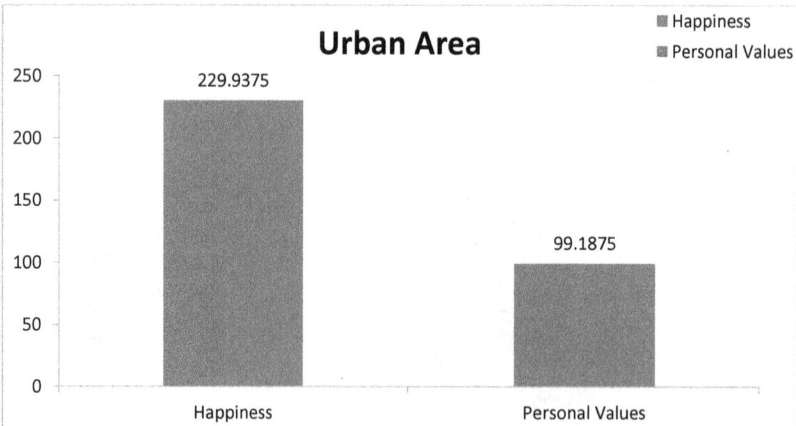

Graph No- 36 shows that the happiness and personal values of urban area at happiness is higher than personal values.

Table-4.37

Showing Mean, 'r' value of Family Environment and Happiness of Rural Area

	Rural Area		'r' value	Level of significance
	Family Environment	Happiness		
Mean	244.20625	239.925	0.510439	0.01
N	160	160		

*0.05 Table value=0.161

**0.01 Table value=0.210

The table shows mean score and 'r' value of both family environment and happiness of rural area. The mean score of family environment is 244.20625, the mean score of personal values is 239.925, the 'r' value is 0.510439 which is significant at 0.01 level. So there is significant correlation found between score of family environment and happiness of rural area. The correlation between family environment and happiness was found positive. Hypothesis No 37 "There will no significant correlation between score of family environment and happiness of rural area." is rejected.

Graph 4.37

Showing Bar Graph with Mean scores, 'r' value of Family Environment and Happiness of Rural Area.

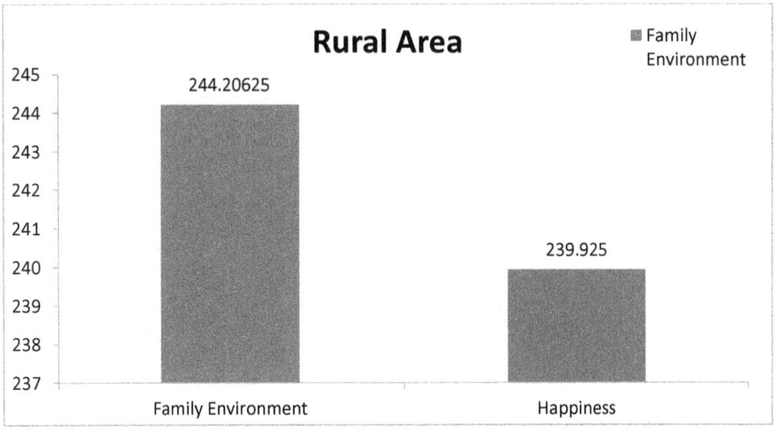

Graph No-37 show that the family environment and happiness of rural area at family environment is higher than the happiness.

Table- 4.38

Showing Mean, 'r' value of Family Environment and Personal Values of Rural Area

	Rural Area		'r' value	Level of significance
	Family Environment	**Personal Values**		
Mean	244.20625	98.68125	0.512766	0.01
N	160	160		

*0.05 Table value=0.161

**0.01 Table value=0.210

The table shows mean score and 'r' value of both of family environment and personal values of rural area. The mean score of family environment is 244.20625, the mean score is personal value is 98.68125, the 'r' value is 0.512766 which is significant at 0.01 level. So there is significant correlation found between score of family environment and personal values of rural area. The correlation between family environment and personal values was found positive. Hypothesis No 38 "There will be no significant correlation between score of happiness and personal values of rural area" is rejected.

Graph 4.38

Showing Bar Graph with Mean scores, 'r' value of Family Environment and Personal Values of Rural Area.

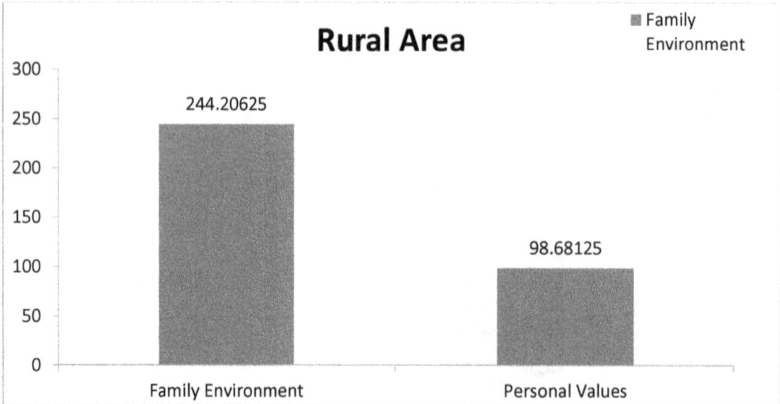

Graph No 38 show that the family environment and personal values of rural area at family environment is higher than the personal values.

Table- 4.39

Showing Mean, 'r' value of Happiness and Personal Values of Rural Area

	Rural Area		'r' value	Level of significance
	Happiness	**Personal Values**		
Mean	239.925	98.68125	0.357111	0.01
N	160	160		

*0.05 Table value=0.161

**0.01 Table value=0.210

The table shows mean score and 'r' value of both of happiness and personal values of rural area. The mean score of happiness is 239.925, the mean score of personal values is 98.68125. the 'r' value is 0.357111 which is significant at 0.01 level. So there is significant correlation found between happiness and personal values of rural area. The correlation between happiness and personal values was found positive. Hypothesis No 39 "There will be no significant correlation between happiness and personal values of rural area" is rejected.

Graph 4.39

Showing Bar Graph with Mean scores, 'r' value of Happiness and Personal Values of Rural Area.

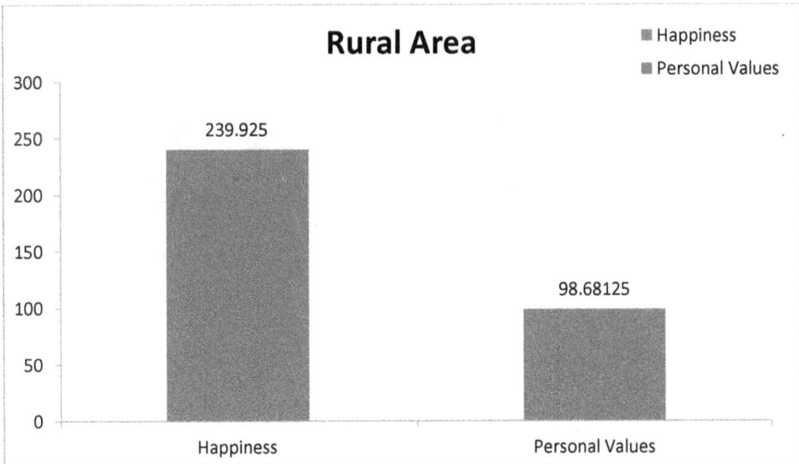

Graph No-39 shows that the happiness and personal values of rural area at happiness is higher than personal values.

4.3 SUMMARY:

After examining all the hypotheses in the present research, we come to the certain conclusions. From the discussion and presentation of information we can see that, total 39 hypotheses various variable tested in the present research that the 30 hypothesis were rejected 09 hypotheses were accepted.

The next chapter-5 summarizes the research work and presents the conclusions and the limitations of the study. Here are some suggestions for further research and utility of this study.

CPSIA information can be obtained
at www.ICGtesting.com
Printed in the USA
LVHW012112291122
734192LV00014B/632

9 781805 451884